The Art of Working with Leather

The Art of Working with Leather

Steven M. Edwards

Chilton Book Company
Radnor, Pennsylvania

Designed by Cypher Associates, Inc.
Manufactured in the United States of America

Library of Congress Cataloging in Publication Data

Edwards, Steven.

The art of working with leather.

Bibliography: p.

1. Leather work.   I. Title.
TT290.E38   685   74-7145

ISBN 0-8019-5831-8
ISBN 0-8019-5837-7 (pbk.)

All drawings are by the author. All photographs are by the author unless otherwise indicated. Glossary courtesy of Tanners Council of America.

On dedication page, Christopher R. Edwards wears an aviator's helmet of 3-ounce chrome-tanned chocolate brown garment cowhide, with star findings.

To my son Christopher,
whose presence
marks our development

Preface

Leather as a medium of expression, whether purely artistic, utilitarian or a harmonious combination of the two, is a versatile, durable and pleasing material. Almost everyone is attracted to leather and leather goods because of their richness of color, texture and feel. And someone is always commenting that he "loves the way it smells."

Leather has been used for centuries in clothing, accessories and carrying cases of all kinds and has always been heralded as a luxurious material, whether in the form of the ermine-trimmed robes of medieval England's hierarchy or in a handbag of contemporary design.

The tanning of leather is a fascinating technological feat, whereby the skin of nearly any animal is refined, preserved and made ready for use. Through controlling many variables, the tanner develops desired qualities in a given skin. From antelopes to zebras, skins are gathered and tanned. Some animal skins, like lizard and kangaroo, have relatively few uses, so the demand is small. But other leathers, like cow and horsehide, calf and pigskin are used in the production of everything from fine gloves to shoe parts to machinery belting.

This book is written for people who want to learn about making leather goods. With both amateur and professional leatherworkers in mind, leather and how to work with it is covered from many angles.

The first chapter on the nature of leather should give a good background. The chapters on tools, materials and construction procedures will give a clear understanding of what tools are available and how to use them. Throughout the book, there are explanations of many ways of working with leather, including molding, bonding, sewing by machine and by hand, tooling, making your own patterns and more.

The second half of the book deals with specific articles and how to make them. However, rather than presenting strict guidelines, I've given ideas and insights which only experience can teach and I've shown as many variations as possible to help the reader harness his own creativity.

The appendix includes a glossary of leathers and related terminology and a list of suppliers for most of your needs.

With so many types and weights of leather, and so many ways of working with it, leather becomes a vital, intricate, enjoyable and functional craft. It is hoped that through this book a direction and understanding can be gained by the leatherworker. Instructions, plans, hints and ideas for many items are given here; these are intended to be used as a starting point—a stimulus and an inspiration for the handworker's own interpretation and expression.

Acknowledgments

Thanks are due many people for helping me make this book a reality. Without flourish or ceremony, they are:

Crissie Lossing, who initiated the whole thing

Jeff Brooks, for advice and counsel

John Beckelman, who straightened out crooked sentences

Robert and Lois Edwards, for help and support in many ways

My wife Nancy, for her clear-sighted ideas and recommendations

Reba Wertentheil and Barbara Bullock of the American Crafts Council

Mrs. Margaret W. M. Shaeffer of the Jefferson County Historical Society

The New England Tanners Club

The Tanners' Council of America, Inc.

And all the craftsmen with whom I've had the pleasure of corresponding, some of whose work is represented herein.

Contents

List of
Black-and-White Illustrations

List of Illustrations

List of Color Illustrations

The Art of
Working
with Leather

Chapter 1
The Nature of Leather

Leather is the preserved, processed skin of an animal, a by-product of the meat, dairy and wool industries. The selling price of an animal to the slaughterhouse, or packer, is very nearly equal to the selling price of the meat. Therefore, all profits and expenses must come out of the sale of the by-products, which include the bones and hooves for making gelatin, the hair for stuffing furniture and the skin to be made into leather. The value of the skin is approximately 5 to 10 percent of the value of the meat.

Technically, a "hide" is the raw or preserved skin of a large, mature animal. The hide often weighs 30 pounds and measures an average of 40 square feet (example: cowhide, horsehide). A "kip" is the skin of a smaller animal, or an immature larger animal. A kip weighs 15 to 25 pounds and measures an average of 12 square feet. A "skin" is the skin of a small animal. It averages 15 pounds and measures about 7 square feet (example: sheepskin). For our purposes, "hide" and "skin" will be used interchangeably.

So what are we working with? A soggy, evil-smelling, distasteful by-product? Of course not. The production of leather by industry is one of the greatest and oldest examples of craftsmanship. From a very crude material, a fine, luxurious one is developed—one whose natural beauty has been enhanced and one which lends itself very well to many purposes.

Nearly 100 million skins are tanned annually in the United States. Close to 25 percent of this amount is cowhide side leather (see Glossary). About 10 percent is calfskin, 15 percent is goat and kidskin and about 30 percent is sheep and lambskin. The balance is made up of a variety of other skins, including horse, walrus, water buffalo, pig, deer, kangaroo, ostrich, seal, shark and so on. Each skin has different qualities; and each can be cut, tanned and processed to yield a very wide variety of leathers. These leathers are used in industries which manufacture gloves, shoes, suitcases, clothing and other items and employ nearly 400,000 people. In addition to industrial uses, the amount of leather used by private handcrafters is growing yearly.

21

	Bags: suitcases, briefcases	Bookbinding	Buffing wheels	Chamois	Fancy leather	Gloves and garments	Harness leather: saddles, collars, bridles	Hats: caps, sweatbands	Helmets, gas masks	Machinery & belting leather	Moccasins	Personal: belts, wallets, handbags	Rawhide and parchment	Scabbards, holsters, laces, razor strops	Shoe parts: uppers, lining only	Shoe parts: uppers, lining, soles, heels, insoles	Sporting goods: balls, gloves
1. Cattle group																	
Steer, cow, bull	X					X	X			X		X		X		X	X
Kip						X						X			X		
Calfskin	X	X				X		X	X			X	X		X		
2. Sheep & lamb group		X		X		X		X		X			X		X		X
3. Goat & kid group	X	X			X	X						X			X		
4. Equine group (horse, ass, colt)	X					X								X		X	X
5. Buffalo	X		X		X							X				X	
6. Pig & hog group	X				X	X	X								X		X
7. Deer group					X	X					X				X		
8. Kangaroo group	X														X		
9. Aquatic group																	
Seal, sea lion, walrus	X		X		X												
Shark, whale	X				X										X		
Alligator	X				X								X		X		
10. Miscellaneous																	
Ostrich	X				X							X					
Lizard, snake, frog					X							X			X		

Figure 1-1 Chart of leather uses.

Leather Selection Guide

You can select leather which is suitable for whatever use you intend by combining necessary qualities from each of four considerations: weight, tannage, type and cut.

Because a leather is very thick, it is not necessarily heavy and dense, although it may be. Nearly any leather can be made to accept water readily, to be water-resistant, to be hard or soft, depending on how it is tanned and finished. Almost any quality can be developed in a variety of leathers during the tanning by removing undesirable constituents and enhancing or introducing desirable ones.

Figure 1-3 This 6-ounce vegetable-tanned leather fire bucket was used to hold sand by the fireplace. It was hardened in the ancient style of *cuir bouilli*. Note the burred copper rivets. Older, handsewn fire buckets were caulked, sometimes with pitch, so that they would hold water. (Courtesy of Jefferson County Historical Society, Watertown, New York)

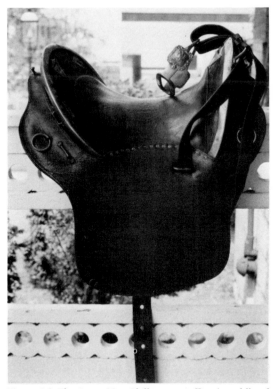

Figure 1-2 The Army Mac Clellan type officer's saddle of Major General Joseph Hooker, ca. 1860. Black 5 to 7-ounce cowhide, trimmed in brass. (Courtesy of Jefferson County Historical Society, Watertown, New York)

The *weight* is the thickness of a leather and is gauged in irons or ounces. An iron = $\frac{1}{48}$ inch, an ounce = $\frac{1}{64}$ inch. Theoretically, one square foot of 4-ounce leather will weigh 4 ounces. While a thick leather, for example, 8-ounce, would tend to be harder than a thinner leather, this is not always true.

23

The following is an indication of actual thicknesses and typical uses:

2 to 3-ounce	▬▬▬▬▬▬▬▬▬▬	wallets, watchbands
4 to 5-ounce	▬▬▬▬▬▬▬▬▬▬	bags, suitcases
6 to 8-ounce	▬▬▬▬▬▬▬▬▬▬	bags, belts
9 to 12-ounce	▬▬▬▬▬▬▬▬	shoe soles

The *tannage* means by what system and with what agent the leather was preserved (vegetable, chrome or oil). The leather's consistency (durability, water resistance, flexibility) is determined by the tanning system, the finishing and the animal from which the skin came.

The *type* of leather means from what animal the skin came. Just as the meat of various animals is different, so too is the skin.

Cattlehides (calf, kipskins and steer, cow and bull hides) are very versatile and durable and are the most commonly used leathers. These hides may be split to make 2 to 12-ounce

Figure 1-4 Leather bound books. Largest is 14″ × 22″ × 4″; smallest is 3″ × 4″ × ¾″. The bottom ledger is from the First National Bank of Watertown, 1860-1868, bound in brown calfskin and suede with gold lettering and designs. The second is the Jefferson County Centennial Register, 1905, bound in red leather. The third, bound in brown suede is Erwin's Store Cash Book, Stone Mills, New York, 1814-1829. The small clasped book, in delicately embossed black leather is a bible, Oxford University Press, MDCCCLIII. The larger, unclasped book is an updated family photograph album, in tooled and embossed brown leather. (Courtesy of Jefferson County Historical Society, Watertown, New York)

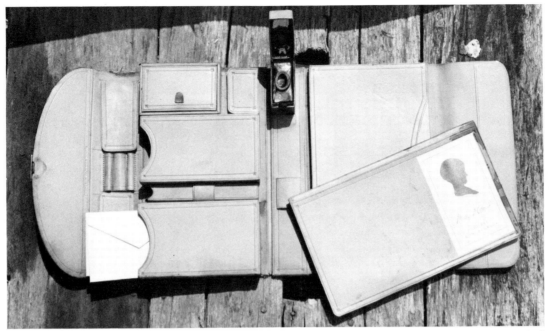

Figure 1-5 A beautiful calfskin writing case from Tiffany's, New York City, ca. 1900. Complete from envelopes to inkwell, the silhouette is of the original owner, Milly S. Baird. (Courtesy of Jefferson County Historical Society, Watertown, New York)

garment or sole leather. Of uniform structure, it dyes nicely.

Sheep and lambskin are generally 2 to 4-ounce and are made into very fine garment leathers. They may have hair or not and are sometimes made into fancy leathers.

Goat and kidskins are thin (2 to 3-ounce) and dense and are excellent for garment and glove leathers. They are usually vegetable or oil-tanned.

Equine hides (horse, colt, ass, mule, zebra) are particularly durable and fine leathers. They are similar to cowhides in texture and thickness.

Pigskin is thin (2 to 4-ounce) and is generally considered to be of inferior quality when it is from a domesticated hog. However, skins from the hog family, for example peccary and carpincho, produce fine glove and fancy leathers. The leather is evenly textured, but is pierced by hair follicle holes.

Deerskin (deer, reindeer, antelope, gazelle, elk) is very fine soft leather, often tanned into buckskin.

The *cut* refers to the way the hide has been divided. Refer to Figure 1-6 and note the *side*, about 22-square feet, one half of the full hide. Sides are good for all bags, belts and large work and are medium priced. The *shoulder*, 12-square feet, is rectangular and straight-sided. This is an economical buy yielding a minimum of waste, but the leather often bears wrinkles from what was the neck. The *bend*, 15-square feet, is a very good piece of leather which is of consistent high quality (and is accordingly priced). The *belly*, 10-square feet, is a cheaper, stretchy piece. Special leathers, such as *French backs* or *English double butts*, are excellent but expensive. The name indicates not only the part of the hide, but has also become representative of a certain combination of the four variables mentioned.

25

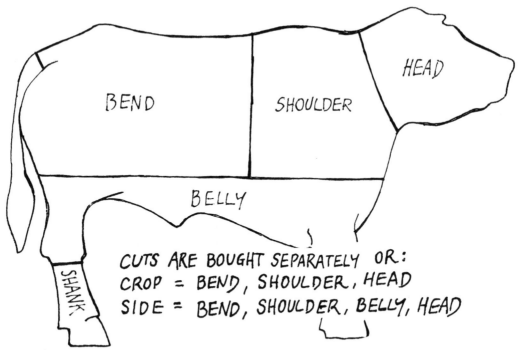

Figure 1-6 Division of the cow into cuts for leather.

Treatment of Hides

Animals are slaughtered by sanitary and humane means and the meat and by-products are processed as quickly as possible. In the "take-off," or removal of the hide from the carcass, great care is taken to avoid cuts which lessen the value of both hide and meat. Like the meat, the hide will spoil if left unpreserved. The meat is kept at the slaughterhouse to be processed and the by-products are sold to various companies to be made into a multitude of products. The hides are bought by a tannery usually in lots of 1,000—a quantity which weighs about 25 tons. The hides are "cured" at the slaughterhouse. They are heavily salted and are thereby temporarily preserved because the salt prevents bacterial growth. Hides are salted in one of two ways: wet-salting or brine-curing. The former consists of spreading 10 to 15 pounds of salt on the flesh side

of each hide in a pile of as many as forty skins. The latter is a modern innovation and involves soaking many "raw" or "green" hides in a bath of salt brine which is constantly agitated. From here on, all work on the hides is done at the tannery.

TANNING

WET OPERATIONS
The following are tanning processes which are performed while the hide is wet and still technically untanned.

Trimming and sorting are the first stages the cured hides go through wherein they are prepared for further processing. The heads, tails, shanks and other perimeter areas are trimmed off; and the hide is cut in half down the backbone for easier handling. Two "sides" are formed by this cut, each measuring about 22 square feet. Lots or "packs" of sides weighing 5,000 to 10,000 pounds are made up; and all the skins in it are tanned and processed identically.

Soaking restores moisture which was lost during the curing. The sides are soaked in huge paddle vats in water that contains a wetting agent and a disinfectant which wets, softens and cleans the hides. The paddles constantly move the hides so that they absorb water evenly for about 10 to 20 hours.

Fleshing is the removal of undesirable flesh, fat and muscle from the flesh side (or inside) of the hide. The grain side (outside) of the hide still retains hair at this point. This process was once done by hand with a scraper over a beam; it is now done by a machine which must be carefully hand-fed.

Unhairing is a chemical process whereby the hair and epidermis (outer layer of skin) is removed. Hides are again soaked in paddle vats; this time in a solution of calcium hydroxide (hydrated lime). Hot water, high lime concentration and rapid agitation quickly dissolve the hair. If the hair is to be reclaimed for any commercial use, a weaker solution and lower temperature are used and the hair is scraped off mechanically.

Bating removes residual, or leftover, unhairing chemicals and nonleather-making substances. The hides are hairless and relatively clean at the end of the unhairing process; but the alkaline materials used in unhairing are still present and must be removed, as must be nonleather-making substances including hair roots and pigments. Next, the pH, or acid-alkaline condition, is adjusted. Addition of salts like ammonium sulphate and ammonium chloride convert the residual lime used in unhairing into soluble compounds which can be washed out. The deliming adjusts the pH to the proper point for receiving the bate, which is an enzyme like that found in animals' digestive tracts. The bate attacks and destroys the remaining undesirable constituents of the hide, which is then thoroughly washed.

Pickling transforms the hide into an acid environment so that it will receive the tan. The pH is again adjusted. A low pH (acid condition) is developed because the tanning agent will not affect leather with a high pH (alkaline condition). Salt and sulfuric acid are most commonly used in the pickling, which is a crude tannage in itself.

Tanning is the conversion of the raw hide into a stable, durable material which will not deteriorate. The raw collagen (leather-making) substances are, by tanning, converted into stable, nonputrescible ones. Also, tanning enhances many of leather's properties: its resistance to scuffing, chemicals and heat and the ability to retain its flexibility after repeated wettings and dryings. After a careful examination of the pH of the pickled hides, a tanning agent is prepared and is introduced to the gently agitated hides. After several hours to several days penetration, the hides are again thoroughly washed.

There are principally three types of tanning which are commonly used today, alone or in combination, to achieve various qualities.

Vegetable tanning is performed with natural vegetable extracts. The bark or wood of certain trees or plants, notably chestnut, oak and quebracho from Argentina, is chopped up and boiled to obtain an extract rich in tannic acid. This is the oldest and most time-consuming type of tanning still in popular use today. Vegetable tanning yields a mellow, moldable leather which is the only tooling leather suitable for many articles. It won't stretch when dry, but can be manipulated and molded when wet.

Chrome tanning is a method which relies on chromium salts to effect a tan. The speed with which chrome-tanned leather can be produced makes this the most common method of tanning in leather manufacture today. This tanning yields a nearly waterproof, but stretchable, leather. It is a soft yet usually heavy leather which has a finish and tends to be spongy around the edges.

Oil tanning preserves the skin with various fish and animal oils. An extremely durable, though soft and flexible, leather is rendered. This leather will often withstand repeated wettings.

27

Until they are actually tanned, all leathers are treated very nearly the same. But with the tanning and the successive processes, the handwork of the tanner is of prime importance. Hundreds of different types and weights of leather can be produced, depending on the application of the following steps. Here you will see how leathers are custom-made.

Wringing removes excess moisture from the tanned, but unfinished, hides on the same principle as a clothes wringer. This step, like many others, is a preparatory one for the subsequent process.

Splitting and shaving give hides a uniform thickness. Leather is split horizontally with a huge blade into two or more layers. Industry demands uniformity and the thickness of the leather must be adjusted and made equal throughout the skin. Only the top layer of the leather after splitting is called "top grain"; and the lower layers, which have no grain, are called "splits" and are most often made into suede. Splits may be sanded or shaved to minimize thickness irregularities.

Retanning, using another agent, may be necessary to impart certain qualities to the leather. This process takes about 2 hours and ensures a maximum of desirable qualities present in a given leather.

Coloring is performed with aniline-type dyestuffs, which are derived from coal, in a rotating drum to avoid streaking and to ensure even, permanent penetration. Most leather is colored to some extent.

Fat-liquoring lubricates the much-processed fibers to give them permanent flexibility upon drying. This process, the last of the "wet operations," is very significant and greatly affects the leather's flexibility and hardness. Leathers which have been identically processed up to this point can be made into hard ski boot leather or supple casual shoe leather by the selection and application of different types and amounts of fat-liquor.

DRY OPERATIONS

The leather is now completely tanned. Operations are now performed to develop special qualities.

Setting out smooths the grain, stretches the skin and squeezes out excess moisture.

Drying removes all but equilibrium moisture. Skins are held by any of several methods and are run through a drying oven. They may be hung over a bar like clothes on a line, toggled with clips to a horizontal screen or pasted to a stainless steel or glass surface with a starch paste. Skins are dried 4 to 6 hours and at the end retain a normal 10 to 12 percent moisture.

CHARACTERISTICS OF THE THREE MAIN TANNING SYSTEMS

	Vegetable Tan	Chrome Tan	Oil Tan
Texture	Even throughout, moderately dense	Pronounced finish, softer in middle	Very soft
Surface	Even, minimum finish	Heavy finish	No finish, has nap both sides
Feel	Mellow, very "leathery"; dry	Slippery, plastic	Very soft, dry
When wet	Darker colors, bubbles, slightly slippery, moldable	No change	Darker color, becomes very limp, stretch increased
Stretch	Almost none, except when wet	Stretches, stays stretched	Extremely stretchy

Conditioning (wetting back) reintroduces moisture, but in controlled amounts. The temper, or softness, is in part determined by the moisture. A fine mist brings the moisture content to 25 percent, and the skins are allowed to mellow overnight.

Staking mechanically softens the leather. Elbow grease has been replaced by a machine which mechanically flexes the leather fibers to give added softness.

Buffing is a cosmetic step. The grain side is lightly sanded to minimize discrepancies. "Full grain" leather is not buffed. One unique quality of leather is that it has natural grain and imperfections, such as barbed wire scars. Leather is, however, a raw material for industry; and these discrepancies must be minimized without being done away with. The handcraftsman can use these "imperfections" to good advantage, since rigid uniformity is not one of his goals. A brand scar which must be strictly avoided by industry may serve as a unique design when built into the flap of a handbag.

Finishing is the application of a film-forming material to the grain of the leather. It must be durable, flexible, adhesive; and it must increase the beauty of the leather. While fine leathers get little finish, all leathers get some as a protective and beauty-enhancing measure. In the past, shellac, albumin, wax and linseed oil were used as finishes. Acrylate, vinyl and polyurethane are currently being used. The finish is sprayed, flowed (poured) or brushed on.

Plating smooths the finished grain surface. Artificial texture can be produced at this stage. Heat and pressure (225° and 300 tons per square inch) result in a smooth surface. Artificial grains are developed by embossing or boarding (rolling the leather's grain against itself). Take a good look at Aunt Hattie's alligator bag—it's really sheep.

Measuring accurately gives the size of the hide in square feet. A hide is very irregularly shaped and is difficult to measure by hand. A measuring machine called a planimeter measures quickly and accurately. A hide is put through the machine, where it trips a number of finger-like projections which take an accurate reading of the whole skin. The size is then stamped on the flesh side in whole and quarter feet. Twenty-one and one-quarter feet is marked 21^1; 21^2 means twenty-one and two-quarter (or one-half) square feet; 21^3 means twenty-one and three-quarter square feet.

Grading is the final step; here the quality of the finished product is determined. Leather is graded according to temper, uniformity of color, thickness and the extent or measure of any surface defects. The leather is then packed in groups of four to six hides, wrapped in heavy paper and labeled.

Today's commercial tanning process is, as it has always been, an industry wherein a careful balance of moisture, acidity and alkalinity, chemicals, good taste and craftsmanship is mandatory. I hope that through this brief explanation of commercial tanning you can better understand what goes into the production of leather. With this understanding, you can handle leather with more integrity, having learned, in some small degree, of its development and nature.

If you have a good deal of time, and especially elbow grease, you may wish to try tanning your own hide by hand. Any skin may be tanned: deer, horse, cow, rabbit or other. Good results can be obtained, but the value of the hide will be more intellectual than monetary, since professional quality leather cannot be produced at home without a good deal of time and effort. With the understanding that you are in for a lot of work with questionable results, you may want to tan a hide anyway and there is no better way to understand the process. Tanning your own hide will give you far more insight into leather's properties than any amount of reading.

Treatment of Leather

FINISHING AND PRESERVING

Dyeing is often incorrectly employed as the only surface treatment given many leather articles. A good finish which protects from within and without should be given all smooth-finished, dyed or natural leather goods, especially those which will have heavy use. The following are for smooth-finished leathers *only:*

Neat's-foot oil is often considered the best conditioner and finish because it lubricates and fills fibers. You can purchase it or make your own by boiling cattle feet bones. Apply several generous coats, allowing it to dry between coats. Sometimes one-third lanolin is mixed with the oil to further condition leather. Oil and grease (from animals) or vaseline are also sometimes used to stuff leather for the same reasons and with results similar to neat's-foot oil.

Beeswax too is an excellent conditioner. Rubbed into the edges or applied warm to the flesh side, it will repel water and add years of use.

Saddle soap, made from neat's-foot oil and soap, revives an old finish temporarily, but is better for cleaning leather than for finishing it.

Commercial paste wax seals the leather, shutting out dirt and water. Use several coats and buff to a high sheen.

The application of the above finishing products can be altered. Not all are always used, but when used are generally done so in this order: dye, oil, wax. Oiled hides may be dyed and waxed, or simply waxed. A leather which is to be finished with little or no color change may be saddle-soaped (to moisten) and then waxed. Always condition (oil) after dyeing to replace oils and moisture. Always wax as a final sealer, regardless of previous treatment.

To remove an old finish before dyeing or applying a new one, wash with a minimum of warm water and a mild detergent. You may also scour lightly with fine steel wool. This will remove wax and some oil, but not dye. It will, however, open the grain for further dyeing. Since the grain will be open after the finish is removed, be careful of stains before you apply a new color and finish.

WATERPROOFING

Several excellent commercial waterproofing products are available and can be confidently used on finished leather. Sprays work well, but pastes or goos are excellent. Sueded leathers need special suede products.

There are, however, other more basic waterproofers, again for smooth leathers *only.* Most of the following formulas use some of the finishes and preservatives mentioned above. This is because all oils and greases fill the fibers and repel water. All should be heated to about 125° F before application; leather is dipped or soaked, or the mixture is brushed on. Use a double boiler and always be careful of fire when using heated wax.

1.	petroleum jelly	4 oz.
	paraffin	1 oz.
	lanolin	1 oz.
2.	tallow	4 oz.
	petroleum jelly	2 oz.
3.	tallow	4 oz.
	cod oil	1 oz.
	lanolin	1 oz.
4.	tallow	3 oz.
	paraffin	2 oz.
	neat's-foot oil	1 oz.
5.	beeswax	4 oz.
	neat's-foot or fish oil	2 oz.

CLEANING

Care should be taken to avoid getting leather goods dirty; but once they are, they may be cleaned without too much trouble. Sueded garments or leather can be cleaned with a dry sponge or soft (not wire) suede brush if the leather is only minimally dirty. If the article is very dirty, have it cleaned *professionally!* The cost will be high, but better than having to replace the item, which you will probably have to do if you try to clean it yourself.

Finished leathers, likewise, are easier to clean before they get filthy. Maintain cleanliness with regular applications of saddle soap. Wash soiled finished leathers with mild soap and a minimum of water. Wipe off the soap with a damp sponge and dry the leather with a dry towel. Keep from heat. To clean off alcohol, wipe with a dry cloth and follow with soap and water as above. To remove blood, flood with cold water, then apply soap and water. To remove acid, wipe with rag dipped in mixture of twelve ounces of water and one teaspoon baking soda, then soap and water.

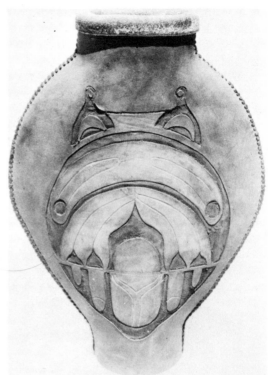

Figure 1-8 This bottle, reminiscent of primitive pottery forms, was molded of vegetable-tanned leather and was handsewn when dry. The design was carved into the surface, and colored wax and aniline dye were applied. By Ron Kwiatkowski. (Photograph by James Utter)

Figure 1-7 This flask was molded, hardened and pitch-lined in the eighteenth century manner. Eight-ounce vegetable-tanned cowhide, rings and linen thread were used. By Scott Nelles. (Courtesy of the artist)

If finished leather becomes very dirty, you may try cleaning it with a bleaching solution of two teaspoons oxalic acid crystals in one pint of water. Apply with a sponge, follow with soap and water, then dry. Whenever water saturates leather, oils are removed and the leather becomes dry. Restore the oil and flexibility by applying neat's-foot oil.

MOLDING AND HARDENING
Just as vegetable-tanned leather is the only toolable leather, it is the only moldable leather. Leather is cased, then pulled, compressed or hammered into shape and weighted down until dry. Simple forms can be hand-formed, but more complex ones require a form or mold, usually made of wood.

The form, which may be used many times, is developed by cutting and sanding wood to the desired shape. Cased leather is stretched over and nailed. In some cases, surface modulation can be gained through modeling with tools; but in the case of a complex shape, both male and female forms are needed. The leather is nailed and clamped between the two until completely dry.

An ancient method of hardening leather can be used in conjunction with molding. Called *cuir bouilli*, literally, boiling leather, it imparts to leather a hardness and durability which can be given no other material in the same manner. The fire bucket in Figure 1-3 was hardened in this way.

A molded piece of vegetable-tanned leather is soaked in cold water until no bubbles rise, then is momentarily soaked in scalding hot water. The piece is then dried over heat. When dry, it will be quite hard, but also brittle. The brittleness can be lessened and water-resistant qualities can be improved by dressing with beeswax.

The combination of moisture, heat and the evaporation of that moisture "sets" the leather's fibers, causing them to become permanently rigid. This is why all leather goods in which rigidity is not desired must be dried in a cool, well-ventilated place.

STORING LEATHER

Leather of any type should always be stored in a dark, dry place at normal room temperature. Sunlight will cause leather to darken or fade; and stored leather, remaining stationary, will end up with irregular dark and light splotches. Dampness may stain leather or promote mold growth.

Sides, shoulders or other large pieces should be made into rolls 8 to 10 inches in diameter, then wrapped in heavy paper. Always roll leather with the grain side *out*. Rolling with the grain in would crush it and cause wrinkles. *Never* fold leather. As many as a half dozen sides may be draped loosely over a large round bar. Be sure there are no wrinkles in the skins. Parts of sides and other smaller pieces may also be rolled, or may be stacked on one another in drawers or boxes. Scrap or very small pieces may be randomly kept in bags or boxes.

Most leathers are perfectly compatible and won't stain each other. Any oiled (*not* oil-tanned) leather must be stored separately, however, because the oil or currying material will seep into and stain other skins.

BONDING

Bonding, or the cementing together of leather surfaces, is very useful in making

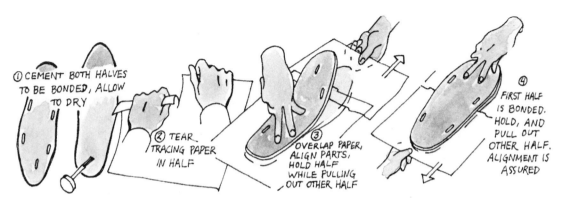

Figure 1-9 When bonding with contact all-purpose cement, be sure of alignment, since you can't move the parts after the initial contact.

Wet rawhide is formed and painted, and beads and fibers are added to complete these "Rawhide Fetish Beads." By Nancy Flanagan. (Photograph by Floyd Flanagan)

Brightly dyed, highly polished, tooled vegetable-tanned leather belt buckles. In each, mirror imagery helps create a strong design. By Barry Olen. (Courtesy of the artist)

A large, exuberantly creative bag of 4-ounce oiled cowhide. The artist employed many techniques from round braiding to filigree and used silver, bone, abalone shell, linen thread and other materials. With enthusiasm and conviction, it has been pulled together into a beautiful, unified piece. By Eugenie Berman.

several different types of leather goods. Shoe soles are bonded together, as are seams and edges in garments. Cementing may be used in addition to stitching or nailing or may be used alone if the strain will not be great, as in a piece of jewelry.

Many types of cement will adhere to leather, but not all are completely satisfactory. White glue, epoxy, rubber cement and others will fasten leather to itself or other materials, but many are not flexible, which is a necessity considering leather's flex, even in the heavier weights. Also, some of these glues do not clean easily, aren't very strong and may even stain leather.

"All-purpose cement," a very concentrated rubber-based adhesive, is available at a shoe supply or leather retailer. This type of bonding agent is the best in nearly every way; for it is very strong, easy to apply, quick, waterproof, nonstaining and the excess is easily removed, just like the weaker rubber cement used for paper. It is, however, flammable.

Both leathers which are to be bonded are given a coat of all-purpose cement on the sides which are to go together. This is a contact or "dry" cement; so one coat, and usually a second, is allowed to dry. Only at this point, after 10 or 15 minutes, are the leathers pressed together, then hammered. On heavier leathers, such as shoe soles, score the adjoining sides with a coarse file, a knife or a special wire brush before cementing to open the leather and allow penetration of the cement. All leathers must be dry, clean and free of grease for successful bonding.

Given two coats of cement, leathers will adhere on the slightest contact and will be very difficult to move or remove. Be sure the alignment is correct before pressing the pieces together. Leather given one coat may be more or less easily moved after initial contact. This is an advantage when basting garment seams or for any sort of "trial run" fitting.

Chapter 2
Buying Materials and Supplies

As we've seen, working with leather is a craft which lends itself extremely well to all types and degrees of involvement. There are hundreds of different leathers, dependent for their distinction on the animal they came from, the way the skin was divided and tanned. Certain leathers are especially suited to a particular use, but the vast majority of leathers have many applications. Leather can be explored minimally, totally or to any point in-between; and professional, rewarding results can be obtained through its tasteful use.

Depending on what kind and how much leatherwork you do, you will need different amounts and types of supplies from various suppliers and manufacturers. To find leather and leather-related supplies, we must look to industry, from which leatherwork as a craft is not yet completely divorced. Good suppliers of materials are, in order of your involvement: a local shoe repair, a leather goods shop, a leather retailer and a tanner. Hobby shops sometimes overprice leather, so compare prices before you buy.

A shoe repairman is a leather expert. He makes his living by fixing leather, mending leather and attaching heels and zippers to leather. He is usually willing to offer advice and sell small amounts of leather, supplies and old tools. He is probably a good source of information to find other suppliers, or you may be able to buy into his next order. Remember, he is an expert, but his living is meagre and is made by selling leather and repairs. His price to you is going to be substantially above the retail he pays. Shoe repairs are visited monthly by two or three leather and supply salesmen. Plan to visit during the salesmen's next stop, and try to order separately, or at least without an exorbitant markup imposed by the repairman.

Don't overlook a professional leather shop for supplies. There you will find well made leather goods and knowledgeable workers. Whether handmade or commercially made goods are carried, these shops often stock enough extra leather and supplies to sell moderate amounts to the inquiring handcrafter. Some companies sell all types of leather goods and have a sideline in a small but diverse selection of tools, supplies and leathers. Remember that here, too, the price to you is a bit above retail. (You pay for convenience—it is much easier to go to a nearby leather shop for supplies than it is to locate and write to a leather retailer, order supplies and be billed.) The atmosphere is one of these professional shops, especially the "handmade" ones, will undoubtedly give the beginner a boost and will allow the more advanced crafter to check his progress. Every shop, whether it sells hardware or flowers, has its own atmosphere. In the successful shops that atmosphere is conducive to buying—because of the stock, the way it is arranged and the decor. Upon entering a leather shop, browse around and inspect merchandise, mood and setting. Gaze freely, touch minimally and try to gain an understanding of what makes those items salable. Maybe you can do better. If you can't, note details and professional approaches which yours lacks. Don't go home and make a copy of what you've seen, but mull over what you've noticed and come up with something better.

Leather

The leather retailer is the one to do business with if you are buying leather in quantities of two sides or more. A few years ago leather retailers were relatively scarce, since few people made leather goods and most of those who did so bought tooling leathers from handicraft companies. But with the current renaissance of crafts, and the increasing popularity of leather as a craft and medium of expression, many retail outlets have been set up. Some are independent, buying from several sources, and some are a part of a large wholesale tannery. Many of these retailers carry a complete line of leatherworking supplies, including literally hundreds of types and weights of leather, a great variety of tools of several grades and sundries such as findings, dye, saddle soap and thread. Some companies specialize in buckles, lace leather or a certain tannage and weight skin.

Tanneries are wholesale outlets dealing in hundreds of feet of leather at a time. They sell mainly to retailers and shoe and boot companies and won't deal with orders under a certain amount. Because of the large amounts of leather sold at one time, a lower price per foot is given to the buyer. In most cases, on a very large order, the buyer specifies what he wants in a leather and the tannery makes it up. But this type of buying is, of course, out of the range of the handcrafter. Handmade leather goods shops can handle these orders financially and can use the leather effectively. The handcrafter cannot, and so must, because of his needs and limitations, pay a higher price at the retailer's outlet, one of which may be annexed to the tannery.

If your involvement calls for transactions with a retailer, start your dealings by looking locally. If that does not prove worthwhile, turn to the List of Suppliers in the back of this book, where you will find a list of retailers and wholesalers and what they sell. Select the one nearest you which sells what you need. Remember that *you* pay the shipping charges. Write to several suppliers and get catalogs and price lists (these usually come separately since prices fluctuate, so ask for both); and then select the one which you feel best fills both your immediate and projected needs. Prices, you will find, are nearly alike, since retailing is a competitive business. Often you may be well advised to deal with a company with a large selection and good service, even if you pay a bit more.

If it is at all possible, visit the retail outlet in person. You will be able to get an accurate idea of what they stock and how they do business. Often a catalogue won't list all their leathers, tools or supplies. Either ask specifically by mail or phone, or visit in person to learn most precisely what is stocked. Visiting in person will also enable you to select the exact skins you are buying. This is mandatory for garment leathers (see Chapter 5, "Garments," for specific guidelines). Leather is priced by the square foot, whether the skin is evenly shaped or not. You are charged for all the appendages dangling

37

from the edges of a skin. Ironically, you are given all the holes and cuts in the middle of a skin for free! Too often I've received leather shipped by the retailer which was totally the wrong weight or color, or which was cut in such a way that it left mostly scrap, rather than yielding usable leather.

After browsing to get an idea of the retailer's stock, get down to business with the salesman or manager. Explain your needs; ask for samples; and ask questions about tannages, weight of leathers, shipping, and whatever else you need to know. Recognize that he is probably the best authority on leathers that you will meet. Buy in quantity if you can. You won't get wholesale prices, but you may get a few dollars knocked off here and there. Join with friends on as large a purchase as you can and ask for a quantity discount. Don't be shy. Leather prices fluctuate daily and the .05¢ per foot he takes off may have been padding in the first place. Compare prices and don't be afraid to haggle a bit.

On this first visit, make yourself known and establish credit if you can. This makes re-ordering much easier. A letter of recommendation from your employer, school or clergyman may help you in this. So might cash on the line. Have in mind what you'll need in the future and express an interest in future, expanded orders from the retailer. Before you leave get the exact name, weight and lot number of the leather or leathers you want now *and* those which you think you will need in the future.

Using this information, you can make your next order by mail or phone. Itemize and use the name, weight and lot number you got the first time. If you have established credit, the retailer will ship your goods "30 days net," which means you have 30 days to pay. This gives you great leeway. If you haven't been able to get credit, the retailer will ship C.O.D., cash on delivery—no money, no leather. It also means that you accept delivery without inspection. Keep shopping around until you find a company which is

relatively near and will give you low prices, fast and courteous service and credit.

This ordering system is fine for repeat orders of the same skin, but often you'll need to order a leather which is new to you and which the retailer may not carry. By selecting a combination of the four leather variables explained in Chapter 1—weight, tannage, type, cut—you can confidently order a leather of which you've seen only a small sample. For example, if you were going to make several tooled leather bags, your order might go thus: one side of 5-ounce vegetable-tanned cowhide. The retailer will probably have this leather, but maybe not in a side. He'll then have to contact you to tell you he doesn't have that in a side, or he'll send two shoulders, which you may not want. It is best to order a certain leather in square feet and allow the retailer to ship to you as he has it: 20 to 22-square feet of 5-ounce vegetable-tanned cowhide. Find a good company with a salesman whose judgment you can trust.

Order findings and tools in a similar manner. Obtain a catalog and price list, then order by code number. Many leather retailers are dealers of very fine tools and carry a respectable line of findings and supplies. While a better selection may be gotten from a company which specializes, it may be easier to order everything at once.

Tools

The production of leather goods has always been primarily a commercialized industry; and so there are many specialized tools, each with a use and specific function in leatherwork. Leathercrafters are fortunate to have these tools of industry, some of which are outmoded in today's large market.

It is possible, as many craftsmen (including myself) have done, to make goods using a pocket knife as your only tool. That is how I made the large traveling bag in Figure 4-23. It was hand-laced; each hole was cut with four separate incisions. Handmade brass buckles set off its design.

But as your skill and knowledge of the material increase, you will see the need for specialized tools to give a smoother, more professional look to your pieces. I am not equating "smooth" in a textural sense with value, but smoothness of design and operation with professionalism. Even very rustic pieces call for the use of several tools, but certainly fewer than are used in the manufacture of highly finished "masterly" pieces.

Build up a continuously growing storehouse of knowledge, leathers and tools. Buy only those tools which you know you will need. When you recognize the need for another, buy that. Don't waste space and money on tools for which you have no need. Having acquired a tool, treat it well. A properly cared for tool will last your lifetime. Oil it, keep it sharp and clean and always protect it from moisture. A set of tools need not be extensive or expensive, but must be functional and useful.

The following, then, are the extensions of your hands with which you will develop your skills and express your ideas in leather.

KNIVES

HEAD KNIFE

Although rarely seen today, this tool was used in harness and handmade shoe manufacture. It is a fine, sturdy, old-fashioned tool which may be used to good advantage by the leathercrafter. The crescent curve of the razor-sharp blade can be used in a rolling, pushing or pulling motion. A versatile knife, it lends itself quite well to cutting very heavy stock and also to skiving. Because of the way it is used, this knife cuts easily and quickly.

MAT KNIFE

This knife, also known as a utility knife, was not designed particularly for leatherwork, but finds its place here quite comfortably. Sharp, stationary, replaceable blades which may be resharpened many times, held in a sturdy grip handle (which holds three or four extra blades inside), make this knife well adapted to long straight cuttings, such as for belt blanks cut from a side, or curves, such as the pieces of a bag. The short, hefty blades bend minimally, so that maximum control is possible.

SKIVING KNIVES

Skiving is the manual thinning of a piece of leather. Used normally at the edges on the flesh side, it is a common practice and is important for a close, nonbinding fit whenever leathers are joined. There are several skives, including the square point, broad point, round point and tapered. Used in various applications, some are sharpened for use at the tip and others along one edge. The tapered skive is the best buy for the handcrafter; it can be used to skive in almost any instance and may also be used to cut patterns like a mat knife.

STITCHING GROOVER

The groover or adjustable groover cuts a groove into the grain side of leathers. In this groove, holes are punched and stitches sewn. The grooved recess protects this seam and keeps it from becoming worn. Some groovers have a guide which keeps them at a set distance from the edge of the leather. Others are adjustable and cut grooves of various widths and depths. Note the stitching on the leather soles of commercial shoes; the stitches are often recessed in a groove cut by this tool. It may also be used decoratively, again on the grain side, to form a pattern or to separate dyed areas (see Figure 4-8b). Groovers may be used on the flesh side, along a fold line, to enable a heavier leather to fold evenly and neatly, without binding.

FRENCH SKIVE

This tool performs the same function in leather that a wood plane performs in wood. In fact, they work on the same principle. A cutting blade is held at the proper angle to cut or shave off leather, or wood. The body of the tool keeps the blade from going too shallow or too deep. The difference between the tools is that the plane's blade is remov-

39

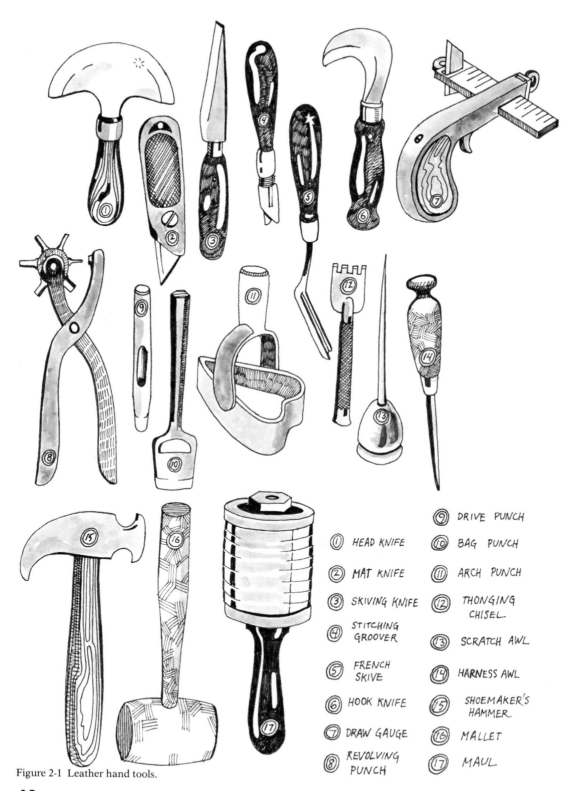

Figure 2-1 Leather hand tools.

9 DRIVE PUNCH
10 BAG PUNCH
11 ARCH PUNCH
12 THONGING CHISEL
13 SCRATCH AWL
14 HARNESS AWL
15 SHOEMAKER'S HAMMER
16 MALLET
17 MAUL

1 HEAD KNIFE
2 MAT KNIFE
3 SKIVING KNIFE
4 STITCHING GROOVER
5 FRENCH SKIVE
6 HOOK KNIFE
7 DRAW GAUGE
8 REVOLVING PUNCH

able, while the French skive is a blade in itself. When this tool is pushed along the edge of a piece of leather, on the flesh side, a strip of leather is removed; that edge is beveled, or skived. This is an excellent tool for joining heavier leathers. It is possible to make the adjoining areas of two pieces of leather only as thick as one, thus reducing binding, bulging and possibly cracking. A skiving knife can perform the same function, but the French skive does it faster, more easily and generally more neatly. (As noted earlier, buy a tool when you need it. You should probably own a skiving knife before you invest in a French skive.)

HOOK KNIFE

This knife is shaped like a linoleum knife, but is made of better materials. Both inside and outside curves should have a good edge, giving this knife many uses. It can be used like a head knife, in the same rocking motion, but the inside curve edge makes this knife unique. It is excellent for ripping out old stitches, such as removing old shoe soles. Don't try to cut with the hooked point, however. The shape doesn't give you the control you need.

DRAW GAUGE

For anyone who will do a moderate-to-large business in any kind of straps, whether for belts or lacing, this tool is excellent. It will lessen your strap-cutting time and effort by half. It is not, however, indispensable. A set-screw holds the heavy razorsteel blade between ¼ and 4 inches away from the pistol-grip body of the tool. The blade, when drawn evenly along a straight edge of the leather, will neatly pare off a clean, perfect strap at the width you set. The advantage is that you needn't measure first, as you must do with a regular blade. The actual cutting goes faster too. Modern draw gauges are cast of iron. They work very well, but are mundane when compared to the draw gauges of 40 and 50 years ago, which were made of tool steel, brass and hand-polished rosewood. Old tools are works of art in themselves. Any craftsman who is lucky enough to have some will tell you so. While technology has brought us more and better tools and materials, the intrinsic beauty of the same has been shattered by mass production, increasing costs and enlarged markets.

PUNCHES

REVOLVING PUNCH

Almost a necessity, this punch will be one of your first purchases. It has a revolving head set with six different-sized cutting tubes which cut six different-sized holes. It is manufactured by several companies in varying qualities. The "basic" revolving punch, priced between $2 and $3, has a ratchet spring and nonreplaceable tubes. A better quality punch has replaceable tubes. When one gets dull or broken, you can replace the tubes rather than the whole punch. The best quality punch costs $10 to $15, has parallel jaws rather than the pliers type, replaceable tubes, a heavy lock-spring to keep the head from moving and a set-screw gauge to ensure that your holes are punched an equal distance from the edge of the leather. Some come with attachments, such as fork punches. The ratchet spring which keeps the revolving punch from turning is the first thing to weaken in a revolving punch. If you are careful not to force the head the wrong way, it will last much longer. With this punch you can rapidly open many holes; but one inherent drawback is that it can be used only on the edges of a piece. Due to the short jaws, necessary for leverage, it has a reach of only about 2 inches.

DRIVE PUNCH

This tool can be used to punch holes around the edges as well as in the center of the work. The drive punch is a single, cylindrical piece of tool steel, the cutting end of which is hollow and sharpened. The hollow gets wider away from the cutting end and a hole in the side allows the passage of the negative circular dots which are removed from the leather stock by two or three sharp blows

41

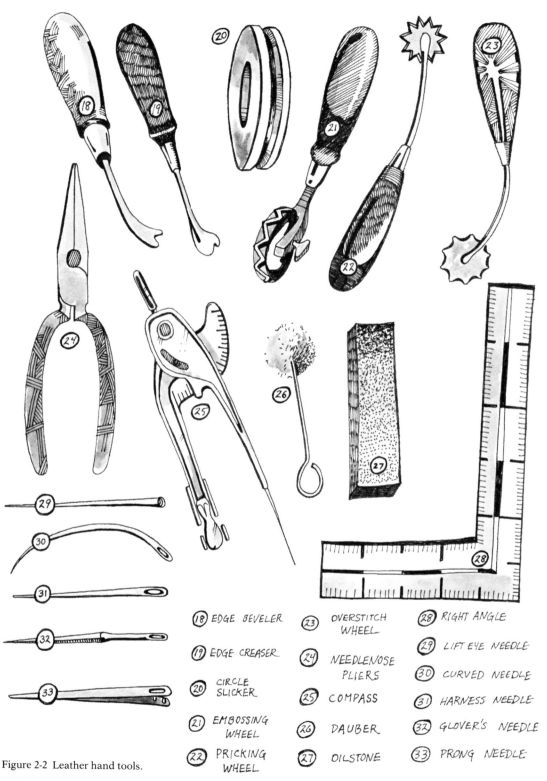

Figure 2-2 Leather hand tools.

(18) EDGE BEVELER

(19) EDGE CREASER

(20) CIRCLE SLICKER

(21) EMBOSSING WHEEL

(22) PRICKING WHEEL

(23) OVERSTITCH WHEEL

(24) NEEDLENOSE PLIERS

(25) COMPASS

(26) DAUBER

(27) OILSTONE

(28) RIGHT ANGLE

(29) LIFT EYE NEEDLE

(30) CURVED NEEDLE

(31) HARNESS NEEDLE

(32) GLOVER'S NEEDLE

(33) PRONG NEEDLE

42

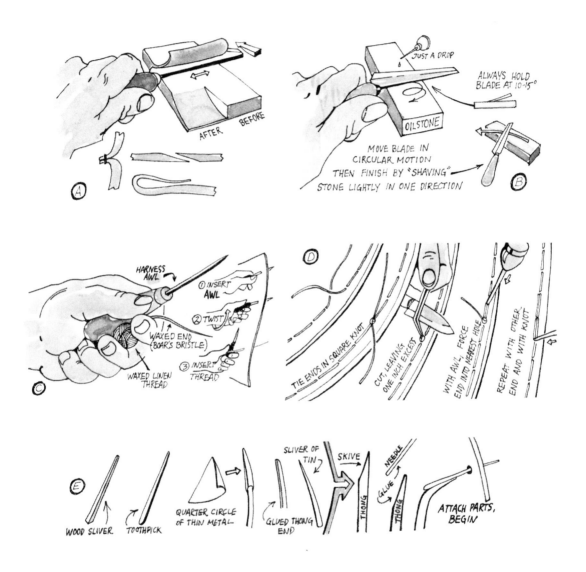

Figure 2-3 Tools and some usages: (a) skiving process; (b) sharpening knives; (c) sewing with an awl, the "old sewing machine"; (d) hiding thread ends; (e) homemade needles for attaching thongs.

43

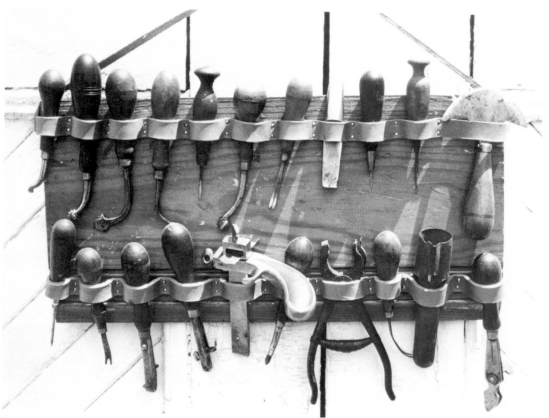

Figure 2-4 Leather tools from another era.

with a mallet. Always be sure that you have placed a piece of sole leather or endstock hardwood under the piece of leather you are punching. One blow on steel and this punch is permanently ruined. While this punch, which comes in many sizes from ⅛ to 1 inch, can be used in places where the revolving punch cannot, use the revolving punch when possible, since it is faster, more accurate and easier to use.

BAG PUNCH

Guard this tool with your life. If you've deemed it necessary enough to spend $12 to $15 on it, you don't want it used in the wrong manner. Specialized and expensive, this tool cuts a narrow oval which can't be made as neatly any other way. It works on the same principle as the drive punch and, likewise,

should be used *only* over sole leather or hardwood. Most common in ½, ¾ and 1-inch sizes, this punch is indispensable for forming buttonholes, holes for the straps in sandals and holes for the tongue of a buckle in belt straps. Buy a small bag punch first. They are less expensive than wider ones and small holes or slots can be strung together to make larger ones.

ARCH PUNCH

These punches are so specialized that they are usually made to order by tool companies. They cut large, identical shapes and are used to make shoe soles and saddle parts, among other things. With a knowledge of steel, welding and tempering, you could make your own. The best bet is to hunt around old hardware and harness shops for no longer used, premade arch punches which you, with your limitless imagination, can utilize. This punch is designed so that the piece of leather which is removed is the one that is used, leaving a negative shape in the remaining leather stock. The drive punch also removes leather and leaves a negative shape (a hole), but the positive shape is discarded and the negative one utilized. As an independent handworker, you are not concerned with conventional applications. You have the freedom to use both negative and positive shapes advantageously, as you see fit.

THONGING CHISEL

This punch is built like a fork. A solid shaft is formed into a series of prongs at the cutting end. Slits 3/32 or ⅛-inch wide are cut by each prong. Leather is not removed, as it is with all the other punches mentioned here. Used in conjunction with narrow commercial lacing, thonging chisels have from one to eight tines (or prongs). While most chisels have prongs which run on the same plane as the body, some are set with diagonal ones which yield a line of slits at a 45° angle to the edge of the work. The more prongs on a given chisel, the faster the work will go; but to go around curves, a chisel with two to four prongs must be used. The eight-prong models are reserved for the straightaways. Even spacing of slits is important,and much harder to explain than to perform. Assume you're using a five-tine thonging chisel. After one blow, remove the tool, which has created five slits. Within the series, the slits are evenly spaced, for that's the way the tool is made. However, you must make sure that consecutive series of slits are evenly spaced. Rather than "eyeballing" it and chancing a mistake, replace the fifth prong in the first slit and strike again. Although you now have only nine instead of 10 slits, you can rest secure in the fact that they are all evenly spaced.

AWLS

SCRATCH AWL

This tool is a valuable marker for leatherwork. Rather than marking indelibly with a pen, it is often easier and always neater to use this awl, the marks from which can be burnished out if necessary. Snub-handled and needle-sharp, this awl can mark lines or holes. Two layers of leather can be marked at the same time by laying one on another and poking with sufficient force. Hole positions are transferred from patterns quite effectively with the tool and it is also useful in handsewing.

HARNESS AWL

Also called a lacing awl, this tool was used extensively by old-time boot and saddlemakers. A sturdy, palm-sized handle holds a (sometimes removable) diamond-shaped blade, 2 to 4 inches in length. It easily slides between and cuts fibers, rather than pushing them aside as does the round scratch awl. Once inserted, a twist will open the slit into a hole large enough for lacing and sewing. This awl can be used blind on the inside of a bag.

Old-timers held the tool in the palm and supported it with the middle, ring and small fingers. The thumb and index finger held a ball of linen thread. Instead of a needle, a boar's bristle was attached to the end of the thread. The bristle was flexible, and some say easier to use than a needle, and certainly less expensive and less rare than needles were years ago. After the harness awl was inserted, twisted and withdrawn, the same hand inserted the bristle into the newly made hole—a primitive sewing machine (see Figure 2-3).

HAMMERS

SHOEMAKER'S HAMMER

This medium-weight hammer has a slightly convex face suitable for hammering leathers without marring or cutting the grain. It is excellent for hammering seams to help bond contact cement. The other end has a strong curve or beak and is very good for getting at small areas.

SQUARE FACE HAMMER

This is an excellent hammer for nailing soles, heels, rivets or any other small work. You can hold the nail and set it with a corner of the face without worrying too much about your fingers. The other end is a round face, sometimes flat, sometimes convex.

MALLET

These come in a variety of weights and are available in wood, rawhide and rubber. While each has a special use, it is best to start with a medium-weight wood mallet. Damp leather can be coaxed into position with a wooden mallet, and seams and stitches can be made to lie flat without smashing them out of shape. Use a mallet on all bag and drive punches, as well as on stamps. A steel hammer will mushroom the heads and could chip them.

MAUL

This is a heavy-duty, heavy-weight mallet used for pounding the larger arch punches home. A short handle is topped by a cylinder made of rings of heavy leather bolted together. Since the hitting surface is round, care must be taken not to miss the mark. Because of the large, changeable striking surface, the maul will last a long time before the rings need replacing.

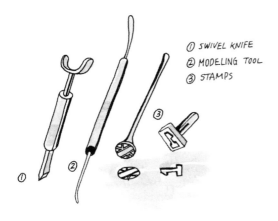

① SWIVEL KNIFE
② MODELING TOOL
③ STAMPS

Figure 2-5 Surface embellishment tools.

SURFACE EMBELLISHMENT TOOLS

MODELING TOOLS

These tools are used to develop bas-reliefs, or a very shallow modeling which gives the illusion of having much greater depth than it actually possesses. Most of these tools are double-ended. They come in a number of different designs; and by using various ones, any configuration may be reproduced on the proper leather.

CARVING TOOLS

These knives are used to emphasize a design formed by another type of tooling. They cut an incision partially through the leather, around a stamped or modeled design, setting it off by separating it from the body of the work. The *swivel-head knife* is held between the thumb, index and second fingers. The index finger rests in a curved head and applies pressure to cut the leather and steady the tool. The second finger and thumb rotate the body and attached blade of the knife for a smooth, unbroken line. The *swivel-tip knife* is used for the same purpose but is held like a pencil. The tip, a sharp cutting blade, swivels 360°, avoiding excessive movement of the work.

STAMPS

Leather stamps are sold by many companies and come in a variety of designs. When placed on moistened, vegetable-tanned leather and tapped with a mallet, a stamp produces an impression which will stay when the leather dries. By positioning stamps differently, a great variety of designs may be obtained using only a few stamps. Since commercial stamps are expensive and the designs are somewhat hackneyed, you may wish to develop your own. Filing brass rods will give you excellent stamps of your own design, enabling you to avoid the cost and standardization of commercial stamps. Brass can be filed easily and will not tarnish or rust, and so will not stain the moist leather.

EDGING TOOLS

EDGE BEVELER The purpose of this tool is to bevel the 90° corner from a freshly cut piece of leather. It is held securely and the beveler is carefully run around the entire perimeter, either on the flesh side or the grain side, or both. This tool gives a professional look to leather goods in two ways. First, it helps minimize a wavy or crooked cut by taking the emphasis away from the 90° edge. Second, it exposes a different side of the leather, which lends a third color dimension when dyeing. The top side of the leather shows the grain one way, the edges show it another and the beveled shoulders show it a third way. When dyed, each exposure of the grain absorbs dye differently, giving you dark edges, darker shoulder and a relatively lighter top grain.

EDGE CREASER This tool also lends a more professional touch to your work. The edge creaser has two smooth, rounded, staggered lips; one rides the edge of the leather as a guide, the other presses a crease, equidistant from the edge of the piece. Edge creasers come in various sizes determined by the width of the space between the lips. Some, called screw creasers, are adjustable with a set-screw. The crease imparted by this tool gives authority to a finished piece and almost says that that crooked cut was *supposed* to be that way. (If it does that for crooked cuts, imagine what it does for straight ones.)

CIRCLE SLICKER A round, flat piece of hardwood or bone with a hole in the middle and a groove all the way around the outside is a circle slicker. The first finger is inserted in the hole; and the edges of a piece of beveled, creased and saddle-soaped leather are vigorously burnished with the groove. The addition of beeswax helps it stay burnished longer.

EMBOSSING WHEEL

While this tool is not restricted to the edges, it is used most commonly there. A decorative motif is impressed into the leather rapidly and neatly when this is rolled along moistened (or cased) leather. Replaceable wheels are available in numerous designs.

NEEDLES

LIFT EYE

This needle is used to sew commercial lacing. The end of the lace is skived, pointed and screwed into a threaded hole at the end of the needle.

CURVED

These come with a variety of shapes, eyes and points. *Round point curved* has a short oval hole and the body is round. *Curved three square point* is the same but the body is triangular. *Curved leather point* has a long oval eye. The eye end is round but becomes triangular at the point end. All these, and others, are nearly semi-circular in profile and are quite easy to grip. They are especially useful for sewing in tight places.

HARNESS NEEDLE

A large eye and blunt point make this needle best for general handsewing in leather. A 2-inch needle is the ideal length. Since holes are rarely poked in leather with the needle itself, a punch or harness awl being used instead, the bluntness of the needle is a benefit. It lessens the possibility of pricking yourself while sewing blind.

GLOVER'S NEEDLE

An exception to the rule, holes are made directly in the leather by this three-sided needle. As in the case of the harness awl, the sharp sides easily pass between and cut fibers. Moreover, the glove leather in which these needles are generally used is quite porous and thin, making this piercing action possible.

PRONG NEEDLE

This is another needle for use with commercial lacing. Again, the lace is skived, pointed and inserted between two studded leaves which clamp it tightly. A bit of leather cement helps it hold.

47

HOMEMADE NEEDLES

In the absence of a commercial needle, you can easily improvise. A toothpick glued to a skived lace will work for a while; or the skived, tapered lace may be dipped in white glue to give it the necessary rigidity. A quarter-circle of tin can be tightly rolled around a lace end for a good needle (see Figure 2-3). Boar's bristles can be attached to waxed linen, as mentioned earlier. This is called a "waxed end" and I refer you to your old-fashioned shoemaker for details.

MISCELLANEOUS TOOLS

PRICKING WHEEL AND OVERSTITCH WHEEL

The pricking wheel marks or, in lighter leather cuts, slits for sewing. You can easily go around corners or along straight edges with this tool; the free-turning wheel is studded with five to twelve points per inch. The overstitch wheel works in exactly the same way, but is used after the stitches are made. It presses them down to finish them. It comes with the same number of points per inch and the two tools are used as a set. Some have removable, interchangeable pricking and overstitch wheels. The older models have a handle which unscrews, revealing storage for spare wheels.

NEEDLENOSE PLIERS

These are pliers which have extremely narrow jaws. They are indispensable for sewing and lacing. A needle can be removed from a tight spot by either pushing or pulling with the pliers. Leather thongs can be pulled through too-small slits by putting the jaws of the pliers through, forcing them open, clamping down on the end of the thong and rapidly pulling it through. Needlenose pliers can also be used to hold nails for hammering, saving your fingers. I know one fellow who uses these pliers to apply dye. A bit of wool is gripped in the jaws, used and discarded.

COMPASS

This tool comes in quite handy for laying out curves, especially in patterns. It can also be used as a divider to roughly estimate equal distances. Get one with an interchangeable

pencil and needle head, so that you can use it like a scratch awl as well as on paper.

DAUBERS

You can buy about a dozen of these bits of wool on a wire for half a dollar and they can't be beat for spreading dye. Use a different one for each color.

RULER

Measure as you work and be sure. You can "eye" some things, but to transfer dimensions or find the middle of a flap for a clasp, measure it. Get a tape measure (preferably a metal, retractable one) for "quickies" and a good steel yardstick for long measures. The yardstick can also be used as a straight edge and as a weight for holding leather while marking or cutting.

RIGHT ANGLE

Any closed form *must* be developed from a right angle in order to be square or true. This angle can be measured on the pattern or the leather; but it is easier, neater and safer to buy a steel right angle. This tool can double as your steel yardstick.

OILSTONE

A dull knife is more dangerous than a sharp one. A small sharpening stone in your tool kit will make it easier for you to keep all your instruments in good condition. Always keep them clean, sharp and oiled. See Figure 2-3 for the correct way to sharpen tools.

Findings

NAILS

"Shoe nails" are similar to finishing nails but are thicker and shorter. Generally they don't exceed ½ inch in length, but are quite thick and have "trumpet" heads. "Clinching nails" are strongly tapered and are very sharp. They are designed to penetrate easily, strike steel and clinch, or turn back on themselves.

RIVETS

These have either a two-part construction or a split end. Both are made of steel and have a coating of brass, nickel or copper which eventually wears off. Rarely, solid copper rivets may be found. Rivets are used to securely fasten parts of a leather item together, or they may be used as pure decoration. Both types come in several lengths for leathers of various thicknesses. All rivets have a shank which is inserted in a hole. The shank of a two-part rivet is fitted with a cap which is set by a hammer blow. A split rivet's shank is opened and flattened, much like a paper fastener. Rivets nicely find their places in holding belts together and holding straps in sandals and bags and are a quick, sure way of fastening.

Grommets and Grommet Setters
Grommets are metal rings which reinforce holes in leather such as holes for shoelaces or drawstrings. They, like rivets, have a two-part construction—the grommet itself and a washer. A flange is driven over the washer and the grommet is permanently set. To perform this, a grommet setter must be used; and each grommet requires a different size setter. I recommend that you see your shoeman to borrow his grommet setter.

Snaps and Snap Setters
Snaps are used in watchbands and all types of clothing, including pants and vests, bags, belts and occasionally in sandals. They are used any time a fairly secure, easy-to-fasten closure is desired. They come in many sizes, with a metal, cloth or leather head. Some may be fitted with cloth or leather to exactly match the piece to which they're being applied. While there are several different types of snaps, the most common is the four-part. Two parts are put together to form one half of a snap. The button goes with the socket, while the eyelet goes with the stud. A snap setter is necessary to spread and hold the parts together and to avoid flattening the domed cap head.

Rings
Rings are a widely used finding. They come in many shapes, sizes and materials. *Loops* or oblong rings, *dees* or D-shaped rings and round rings are used to weight flaps, to join straps to bags and are often used as buckles in belts, sandals, shoes, hats, and most other leather goods (see Figure 2-7). From about ¾ to over 2 inches, these rings are available in many materials, including copper, nylon, plastic, steel and brass. The all-time favorite is brass because it always looks nice, is heavy and won't wear out.

Buttons
Metal, bone or leather buttons of any size or style can be attractive with leather. The best metals for buttons which are applied to leather are pewter, copper and brass. All metal findings, particularly buttons, are subject to heavy wear; and a plated finding soon loses its plating. The best style buttons for leatherwork are those with a shank, since it raises them off the surface of the leather and facilitates their operation. Buttons are used for clothing, watchbands, flaps and adjustable straps. There are many types of braided leather buttons which you can easily make. I refer you to *The Ashley Book of Knots* (see Bibliography).

Buckles
This finding makes possible the rapid, secure coupling and uncoupling of two pieces of leather (see Chapter 4). Basically, there are five different types of buckles. They are: the single bar, the double bar, the single roller bar, the double roller bar and the stud tongue. There is a greater variety of sizes, shapes, colors, materials, weights and finishes available in buckles than in most other findings. Since the buckle is the main focal point nearly everywhere it is applied, don't use cheap buckles. Stamped buckles are cheaper than cast ones and they look it. Solid brass is the best buckle material. Recently, several factories (see List of Suppliers) have begun manufacturing cast brass buckles in every design from reproductions of ancient coins to art nouveau patterns. These are not inexpensive; but in years to come, they may become as valuable as Tiffany's Wells Fargo buckles are now. Sometimes a box of buckles can be bought at an old hardware store for $2 or $3.

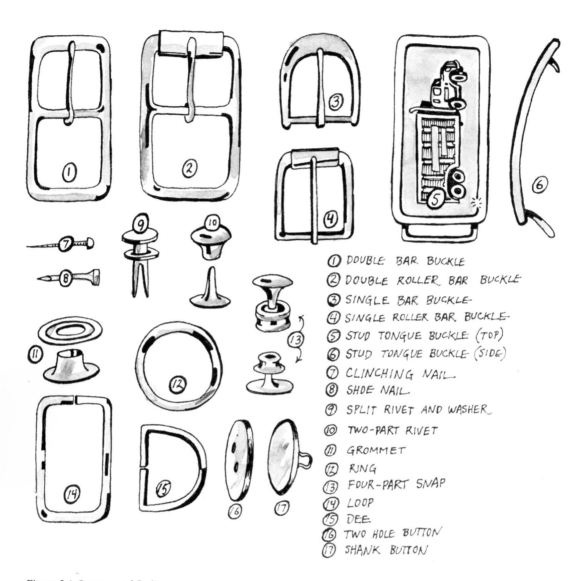

① DOUBLE BAR BUCKLE
② DOUBLE ROLLER BAR BUCKLE
③ SINGLE BAR BUCKLE
④ SINGLE ROLLER BAR BUCKLE
⑤ STUD TONGUE BUCKLE (TOP)
⑥ STUD TONGUE BUCKLE (SIDE)
⑦ CLINCHING NAIL
⑧ SHOE NAIL
⑨ SPLIT RIVET AND WASHER
⑩ TWO-PART RIVET
⑪ GROMMET
⑫ RING
⑬ FOUR-PART SNAP
⑭ LOOP
⑮ DEE
⑯ TWO HOLE BUTTON
⑰ SHANK BUTTON

Figure 2-6 Some metal findings.

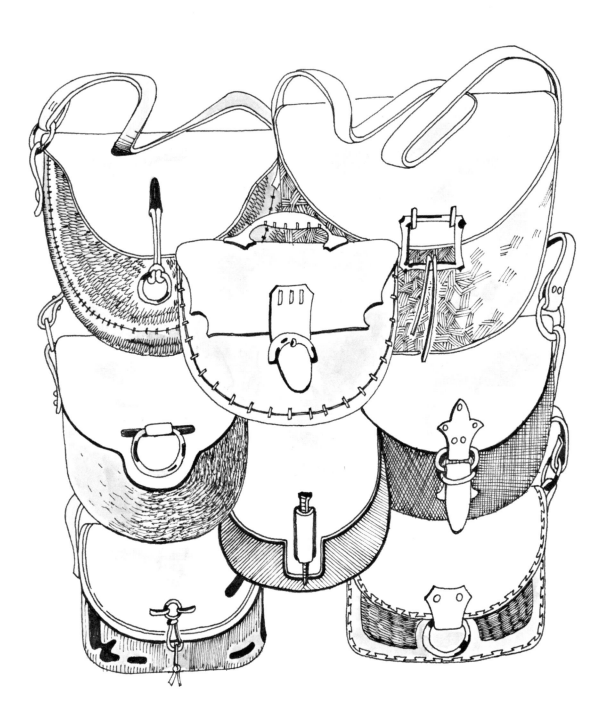

Figure 2-7 Findings make effective clasps.

Dyes, Finishes and Preservatives

DYES

Dye is used to color hides; and if you're not careful how you apply it, it will color your hide.

Equally good results can be achieved with either oil or solvent dyes. They give different effects. Oil (bottled) dye gives a glossy, semi-permanent finish; while solvent dye gives a very permanent but less glossy finish. Many colors are available. They all penetrate leather, coloring not only the grain, but well into the fibers. Dye may be blended either in the bottle or on the hide for a very wide color range, using surprisingly few hues. Dye can be used to minimize or emphasize surface modulation, grain or tooling. Application techniques vary, but all produce a permanent color change in the leather.

FINISHES AND PRESERVATIVES

Many commercial products are sold to finish, preserve and waterproof leather. Although the only commercial products I use are a waterproofer called Snow-Proof, dye and paste wax, most well-known brands of finishes are very good. There are three old-time products which I feel can do the job of any of the newer finishes at much less cost, and maybe better.

SADDLE SOAP

This comes in a tin or a cake and moistens, cleans and finishes all smooth-grained leathers. If you vigorously rub in a couple of coats, wiping off the excess, the leather is unconditionally guaranteed to look better and last longer. Saddle soap restores (temporarily) faded-looking leathers by revitalizing their down-in-the-mouth fibers. It is a mild soap with an oil added. The soap cleans the leather while the oil lubricates the fibers.

NEAT'S-FOOT OIL

This is a fatty yellowish oil made from cattle bones, offal and other animal oils. It is an excellent dressing for any smooth-grained leather, since any oil lost in dyeing or weathering can be restored. This oil also acts as a waterproofing agent.

BEESWAX

This soft yellow wax is pure wax, not doctored and stiff like paraffin. It can be used to minimize frayed edges, to burnish edges and to waterproof in conjunction with neat's-foot oil.

Setting Up a Workbench

WORKING SURFACES

You will need several surfaces on your workbench for various operations. For cutting, a large, smooth, close-grained or grainless surface is excellent. Linoleum, having no grain and being resilient, works nicely. Wood, however, is probably the best cutting surface. Endstock hardwood is ideal; although a hardwood plank, such as an old table leaf, works satisfactorily. Softwoods, such as pine or spruce, have a wide and soft grain, causing the knife blade to get caught and to be pulled off the mark.

For pounding seams and setting nails and rivets, a steel surface is necessary. A large steel plate has the heft needed to withstand heavy hammering and the anvil surface to set nails and rivets. (Don't forget to keep a scrap of sole leather between your drive punches and the steel.) For skiving, a hard, flat, smooth surface is the best, allowing feather edges. An old lithography stone combines these qualities excellently. Tool on a marble slab.

DRAWERS AND SHELVES

When possible, have a rack of shelves in easy reach. Keep your boxes of findings, dye, saddle soap and all other materials handy. An excellent workbench is an old desk which houses at least three or four large drawers and has a surface large enough to work on and to hold a rack of brick-and-board shelving. A much more productive atmosphere is attained if you are totally organized, having all your tools, materials and supplies not more than a few steps away. A handy tool rack can be made by tacking a strap of leather to a board (which gets hung on the wall) or to the edge of your workbench, leaving loops to hold the tools (see Figure 2-4).

LIGHT

Light your work area well, either by natural light or artificial means. You are working with razor knives, expensive materials and permanent dyes. One slip of the knife could permanently end your career as a craftsman. (For removing bloodstains from leather, see Chapter 1, "Cleaning.") A spilled dye bottle can be a horrible, expensive mess.

Conclusion

To be sure, tools are not cheap. But by wise purchasing, you can avoid wasting money and the tools you do buy will last many years. An adequate set for the novice would consist of a knife, a revolving punch and a hammer. Later, start adding edging tools, awls, specialized knives, dyes and finishes if you wish. Use a tool for the purpose for which it was designed and you will have it much longer.

There are many companies which sell tools and, of course, quality as well as the price varies. Generally, I recommend investing in quality tools. A $10 punch is simply better made than a $2 one. Most high-priced tools will last indefinitely, but you may have cause to use them only occasionally. You might argue that the tools you'll use all the time would need to be the best quality, but what about those which you'll use only once a month? Couldn't you get away with spending less, considering how seldom they will be used? However, if a company makes poor standard tools, their specialized tools will be nightmares of production shortcuts! May I give as an example a $1.50 wooden draw gauge which can't cut strips.

Examine tool materials. Be wary of companies whose brass tools are attracted by a magnet or whose "steel" looks like plastic. To get the best pork chops you go to the butcher; to get the best tools, go to a hardware or tool company.

Some of the tool companies in the List of Suppliers are wholesalers and won't deal directly with the public. Request a catalog and price list and they'll include a list of retailers from whom you may buy their tools. Osborne, particularly, makes the finest American leather tools.

Chapter 3
Production of Leather Goods

The tools described in the previous chapter were all developed for the leather industry. This chapter concerns itself with working methods, construction procedures and the use of these tools and materials.

Step-by-Step Procedures

Leather goods are developed much the same way bread is baked by a baker. There are several steps which are always performed. Some are done only occasionally, at the discretion of the handworker and according to the needs of the piece. (Hint: to know proper procedures, know your tools and materials well.)

The production of leather goods involves the following basic steps, sometimes out of order, sometimes omitting (or even adding) some: (1) designing the item, (2) developing the pattern, (3) laying out the pattern, (4) cutting and trimming to size, (5) edging, (6) dyeing, (7) tooling, (8) assembling.

DESIGNING THE ITEM

Design is that vehicle through which a craftsman exercises his individual expression. If your design is unique, functional, easily operable and well-made, you have solved, and even avoided, the problems which are most common for a leatherworker—problems like repetition, making "cute" items, having non-fitting parts, having a confused collection of ideas and being bored with your work.

Once you have obtained your leather, the first step in the production of any leather goods is to develop a design. Your design must be neat, functional, original and within your physical capabilities. Your project starts with an idea: for example, "a large, hand-held bag, with an adjustable strap and two interior pockets, tooled, of natural color." Keeping these desired qualities in mind, your idea develops into a functional design.

The neatness of design mentioned above does not mean sterility of design or idea, nor does it mean a lack of originality. Many crude, rustic bags have a neatness, that is, a unified, well-constructed quality. Edges may be rough, but the pieces fit together; and the bag has what you might call the strength of its convictions. Neatness does mean matched pieces, evenly punched holes, tied and tucked-in ends and easy and quick openings and closings.

Originality of design, while not the most important design quality, is certainly the most striking. This originality is determined by the individuality of conception, design and construction. Variation and innovation are the soul of originality.

DEVELOPING THE PATTERN

Patternmaking is an art in itself; or maybe it's mathematics. Your pattern *must* be true, that is, with exact right angles and straight lines; and your holes *must* be evenly measured, or your piece will have a built-in warp. You must understand how each piece of leather will react to stress and bending upon assembly.

Materials for patternmaking are these: a large steel right angle, a pencil, a yardstick, newsprint and scissors (not to mention thought, skill and patience).

To have a viable pattern, it *must* be true. This means not only having the pattern built around a right angle, but also matching the pieces exactly. Variations of more than ¼ inch cannot be tolerated. By starting with a good pattern, you can avoid sloppy cutting and fitting which is the sign of careless craftsmanship.

After you've designed your piece, make a proportioned sketch to develop scale and size. When you've determined what size you want, begin laying out the actual, full-size pattern on newsprint. Start with a right angle. You may draw one with your steel right angle, or you may start from the pre-cut corner of the paper. You may wish to consolidate as many pattern pieces as you can. Sometimes you can make the front, bottom, back, top and flap of a bag, for example, all one piece. This practice may not save much leather, but it encourages evenness and straight lines and eliminates many seams.

Measure everything. Even if you are working with arbitrary figures, such as when you initially lay out your pattern, it is always easier to work in round numbers. Use your right angle to check all square corners. If you don't you may find that your rectangular pieces have mysteriously become parallelograms, or a rectangle may somehow have become wider at one end. Check your measurements with the yardstick. Make sure all measurements are accurate and take the time to alter incorrect ones.

To draw a curve, you may use a compass, a French curve, a jar lid or you may do it freehand. You may want to duplicate that curve, as in two sides of a symmetrical bag, or in separate parts of a bag to develop secondary design qualities. Draw the curve on the pattern and cut it. Then fold the pattern on the mid-line and carefully copy it on the other half. Mark the vertical mid-line on all pattern pieces before cutting them out. You'll need this line to accurately mark holes.

There are four types of gussets, or side pieces, in a bag and their patterns are developed similarly. (See Chapter 4 "Bags.") They must fit your front and back pieces and should be about 4 inches longer than the distance around the perimeter of three sides of the front and back. This allows a bit less than 2 inches (¼ inch or so is lost due to thickness) to fold over at the corners of the piece. In this fold, you can sew a brass ring to hold the shoulder strap, or leave it plain. The size or length is determined by measuring the perimeter of the front. Carefully roll that pattern piece along the yardstick to find this distance, then add 4 inches. This fold gives design and physical strength. You may wish to make a continuous gusset out of two pieces joined at the middle to save leather. If so, halve your pattern, allowing about ⅝ inch for overlap.

In all handsewing, lacing and thonging, with the exception of sewing in the very lightest of leathers, you will need to punch holes before you sew. It's most important that the holes match in the pieces being sewn together, not only on straight edges but around curves and corners too. (I refer you to the hole-making tools discussed in Chapter 2, the drive and revolving punches and harness awls.)

If you are lacing or thonging pieces together and want the thong to start and finish on the same side (usually the inside), you must have an even number of holes. If you are sewing with thread, the number of holes doesn't matter.

To mark an even number of uniformly spaced holes, take a small piece of paper and mark dots, spaced as you want your stitches, on its edge. I usually sew two or four stitches to the inch with thread and almost always two to the inch with thongs. There are, however, records of as many as sixty stitches to the inch! Using the piece of paper, you will mark holes the way slits are cut with the thonging chisel. The four dots are copied onto the pattern and the paper is moved, the first dot being placed where the fourth one was marked. This ensures overall even spacing.

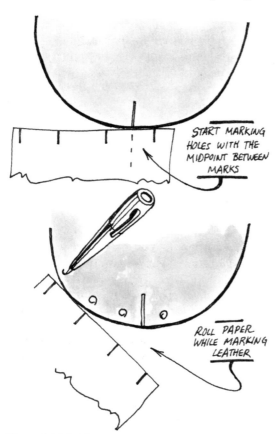

START MARKING HOLES WITH THE MIDPOINT BETWEEN MARKS

ROLL PAPER WHILE MARKING LEATHER

Figure 3-1 Marking an even number of evenly spaced holes.

Start your marking at the midpoint at the bottom of your piece. Place that midpoint *between* two of the dots. With ½ inch stitches, holes should be marked ¼ inch on either side of the midpoint. (see Figure 3-1.) When you go around a curve, roll the paper along the pattern's curved edge, without letting it slip. Keep going until you reach the corner. That last mark should be about ½ inch from the edge. You may have to juggle the marks around a bit, but rather than moving only the last hole, keep even spacing by slightly changing the five or six previous marks.

When you have half of your pattern's holes marked you can fold it over and mark through with a scratch awl. This means identical, evenly spaced holes all the way around. It also means an even number of holes. Take this fully marked pattern piece and mark through again to any identical pieces. Front and back of a bag are generally the same. Pattern pieces should be made for both parts to facilitate laying out on the leather. Mark the holes in the gusset the same way you judged its length. Carefully roll the gusset edge to edge with the already marked front piece, marking as you go. Here again, if you mark only one side you can transfer the holes by folding and pricking. If you do this consistently, you greatly lessen your chances of having unmatched holes. One more hint about holes: they should be between ¼ and ½ inch from the edge. You can draw a line ¼ to ½ inch from the edge all the way around the pattern to be certain of conformity.

LAYING OUT THE PATTERN

Roll out your leather, grain side down, on a clean table or on the floor (see Chapter 2 for purchasing leather). Arrange your pattern pieces. You should have a pattern for every piece, even identical ones, to help you get the best use of the leather. Occasionally, you may want to devote one entire hide to making several identical items. In this case, make several complete, identical patterns. Time consuming? Yes. But leather generally costs above $1 a square foot and, for reasons of economy, you will want to avoid any waste. When using heavier leathers, 4 to 12-ounce, you may lay out your pieces in any arrangement. Lighter skins, such as garment suede, must be laid out with respect to the grain, that is, parallel to the backbone of the animal, so that the grain runs in the same direction on the wearer as it did on the animal.

Arrange your pieces closely. I often butt up straight-edged pieces so that I need cut that line only once. Be careful of wrinkles or waves in the leather, as they are difficult to compensate for, no matter how true your pattern. If the piece of leather is very wavy, try wetting it or weighting it flat with bricks. On all leathers, avoid bad spots, including cuts to grain and flesh sides, abrasions, brands and the edges which in some leathers (especially latigos and suedes) are spongy. Be sure, too, that all your pieces fit the leather.

To mark the pattern on the leather, you can tape it or just hold it, marking around it. I always mark only the beginning and end of a straight edge, completing the line with the aid of a ruler. Patterns made of tin or galvanized iron are excellent, easy and quick to use and are well worth the time they take to make if you will be repeating the same pattern. They are timesavers because you can cut right around them without transferring the lines with pen or scratch awl, as you must do with all paper patterns. I generally prefer the scratch awl to mark patterns, because if I find I've made a mistake or changed my mind, the marks can be burnished out. Always mark on the flesh side, unless you can't see the line you've marked. Only then mark the grain side.

CUTTING AND TRIMMING TO SIZE

With all preparation done, cut out your leather pieces. Use only a very sharp knife and take both positive and negative shapes into consideration. Look at what you are cut-

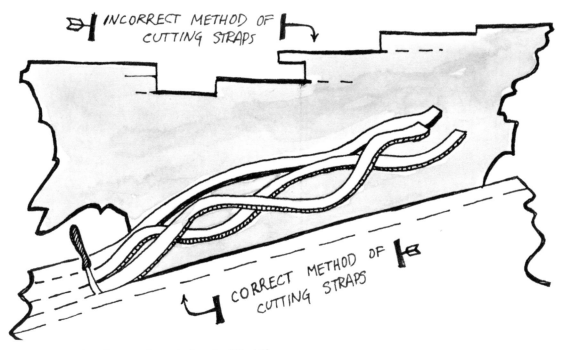

Figure 3-2 Cutting all straps the entire length of the hide to save leather.

57

ting out as well as what you are leaving behind. Don't destroy the latticework of leather between pieces by thoughtless hacking. You may have usable leather, or the beginnings of a wallhanging (see Chapter 6).

Use a continuous stroke and keep your whole arm stationary, allowing the controlled weight of your body to make the cut. Keep the knife perpendicular and avoid cutting into good leather at the end of a cut.

For the sake of economy and ease, I always cut a straightedge along the backbone of a side of leather. Every time I need a strap, of any width, I'll cut one off the entire length. By cutting the length, you avoid wasting a hide in hacked-up pieces. All straps are cut full length and are trimmed to size. Sides are generally 7 to 8 feet long at the backbone, so you can easily get a bag gusset and a belt, three gussets or two belts out of one strap (see Figure 3-2 and Chapter 4 "Belts").

After the strap or pattern piece is cut and trimmed to size, the raw, square, fresh-cut corners or ends should be trimmed. It not only looks better but a rounded corner or end doesn't get caught on things. Both corners can be trimmed with a simple 45° cut. (A strap end is cut with six cuts, see Figure 4-6.)

If your design calls for thongs, you can cut your own, matching or contrasting the leathers and saving money at the same time. Using a mat knife, or ideally a draw gauge, cut ¼-inch thongs from the straightedge. Or, you can cut thongs like the old-timers by cutting a circle or even a square of leather into a long spiral, soaking and stretching it.

EDGING

Finishing the edges on your work is advisable for aesthetic reasons. Edging is performed with an edge beveler, edge creaser and circle slicker. Used in this order, these tools give

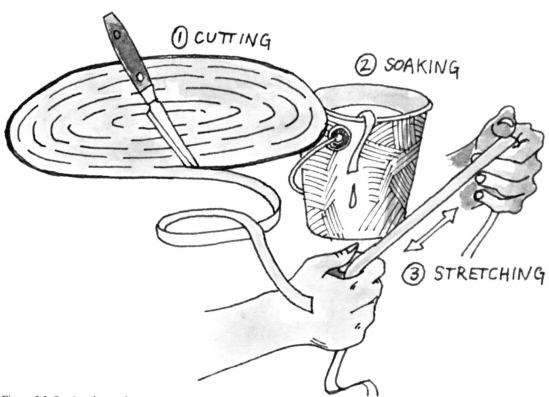

Figure 3-3 Cutting thongs from scrap stock.

58

your goods a smoother, more professional look. The edge beveler, as described in Chapter 2, trims the corner off a freshly cut piece of leather. Used on any leather from 3 to 12-ounce, this tool may be applied to grain side, flesh side or both. They come in several sizes, from #00 ($\frac{3}{32}$ inch) to #6 ($\frac{1}{4}$ inch), (tool size codes may vary with different companies) and are best used before dyeing. The edge creaser, too, comes in several sizes, #1 (about $\frac{1}{8}$ inch) to #5 (about $\frac{1}{4}$ inch). The edge creaser creates a decorative crease around the piece, giving it design strength. This tool is used after dyeing and saddle-soaping and will work best on damp vegetable-tanned leather. It can be used cold, but works best if warmed over an alcohol flame. Both these tools are held firmly by their rounded handles and are pushed in a direct, even manner. Next, burnish the edges with the circle slicker. For best results, first rub a little beeswax into the edge.

DYEING

Dye is applied with any size wool dauber or swab in several directions to ensure even coating and penetration. Leathers may be dyed as they come from the tannery. Any hide will accept dye, but not all will accept it evenly. Streaks and splotches, which you may not find objectionable, are common. (See Chapter 1, Treatment of Leather.)

Dye in two stages. Allow the first coat to soak in completely. The second coat should then be applied (using a dauber, brush or sheepskin rag) and the excess wiped away. Buff until dry. Apply a good paste wax finish to reseal the leather.

Some leathers actually dye better when they are damp rather than bone dry. Experiment; but experiment on scraps to see how various conditions affect various leathers. Don't be afraid of using dye. It can brighten things considerably and can be used to very good advantage. But don't overuse it. Sometimes a natural full-grain cowhide which gets mellower with age is the best solution. The beauty of leather increases with age, while dye has a tendency to fade.

Your dyeing should be done before assembly. If a piece is completely sewn together, you really can't color it evenly. You may want to cut your leather pieces and dye before punching holes; then the holes' interiors will show the color of the leather. If you punch holes and then dye, the interiors will be the same color, but the dye may run through and stain the back.

After dyeing, a finish should be applied to moisten, preserve and protect the leather. Dye not only colors but also dries the leather; and dry leather soon cracks. Saddle soap, neat's-foot oil, beeswax, a combination of the three, commercial waxes or commercial colorant finishes may be used separately or in combination. (See Chapter 1, Treatment of Leathers; Chapter 2, Finishes & Preservatives.)

TOOLING

Leatherworkers generally have similar opinions about tools and their uses and about various leathers and their applications, but they are always at odds about tooling. *"Tooling"* is the term for the most commonly practiced surface embellishment of leather, whether by embossing, repoussé (impressing from behind), incising, cutting into filigree patterns or any combination of the above.

Advocates of tooling claim it gives leatherwork another dimension. It also gives the leatherworker the opportunity to express himself beyond the shape or proportion of the object itself. Tooling also allows the craftsman to spend careful hours producing intricate designs which probably make the finished product more valuable and, hopefully, more beautiful.

Those who denounce tooling say that it is unnatural and unnecessary to disturb the natural beauty of leather—especially the fine calfskin normally used for tooling. They say that tooling actually works against any natural beauty because of its artificiality. But what bothers them most is that tooling normally consists of clichéd concepts and designs (which you may buy and trace) such as

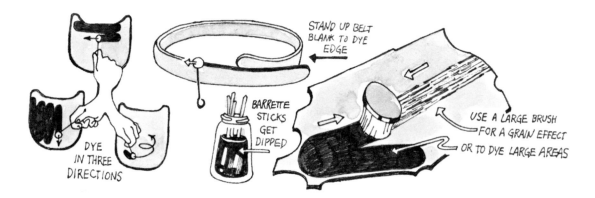

STAND UP BELT
BLANK TO DYE
EDGE

DYE
IN THREE
DIRECTIONS

BARRETTE
STICKS
GET
DIPPED

USE A LARGE BRUSH
FOR A GRAIN EFFECT
OR TO DYE LARGE AREAS

Figure 3-4 Various ways of applying dye.

a hundred variations of "country and western floral," which is practically all you see "round these here parts." Also, those opposed to tooling note that more thought often goes into the decoration than into the construction of the piece itself.

Be that as it may, here's how you do it. Any type of design may be created by tooling, including floral, figurative and abstract designs. Tooling is used on many leather articles, including wallets, belts, handbags, furniture, hats and book covers. It is always performed on vegetable-tanned leather *only!* And it is usually a good quality, fine-grained leather such as calfskin. Vegetable tanning imparts to the leather the quality of readily absorbing water and swelling. Later, after most of the water has evaporated, a design which is pressed in will remain when the leather dries. Chrome or oil-tanned leathers don't have this quality. Various tests can be made quite simply to tell the tannage of a given leather. (See chart of tannage tests, Chapter 1.)

Leather can be dampened in preparation for tooling in any of several ways. It can be sponged from the back until the front starts to darken; it can be sponged or sprayed with an atomizer from the front; or it can be cased, which is the most satisfactory yet most time-consuming method. Cased leather is completely immersed until no bubbles rise—5 seconds to 5 minutes, depending on thickness. The soaking wet leather is then removed and wrapped in a turkish towel for 12 to 24 hours. During this time, it becomes mellow, soft and evenly damp. If it is too wet, that is, if a modeling tool raises a bead of water, you must wrap it longer. Keep it in a closed box or drawer for the casing.

At some point, depending on the leather and its humidity, you will find the leather has become quite limp and will hold impressions. Have your design drawn on heavy paper the same size as the leather and paper clip them together. Using the tracer, firmly go over the outline of the design completely. Remove the paper and faint lines will guide you in continuing your tooling. Always tool on a hard surface such as a marble slab.

Most tooled designs are developed by the use of several tooling systems or processes: by stamping, modeling, carving or all three. (The tools necessary for these processes are dealt with in Chapter 2.)

60

The stamps are positioned and lightly tapped to create an impression. Many designs can be created using only a few stamps. Open ended stamps impart a design which may be combined with, or attached to, another identical or different impression. In this way, one stamp can be a single module with which an entire motif is built. The embossing wheel takes the motif idea a bit farther. It has an etched roller which rolls a continuous design. Thus, it is very handy, especially for borders.

Modeling, I feel, can be the most imaginative type of tooling. Designs are systematically developed through the use of different modeling tools. A delicate or very bold bas relief emerges as the work progresses. For the careful worker, much is possible with this bas relief, which is a 3-D sculpture of very low depth.

Carving of leather is quite effective too. It is used most frequently around the edges of stamped and modeled designs to give them heightened, permanent contrast. Whichever cutting tool is used, a beveled slice offsets the raised, lighter area it surrounds.

After the outline is transferred, the work begins in earnest. The outlines are pressed deeper and deeper, while surface contour is obtained by the subtlest of modulation. Since stamping, carving and modeling are time-consuming and the heat of the hands dries the leather, keep a sponge and clean, cool water handy to re-moisten the work.

There are many other refinements to the art of tooling, for it is a well-practiced art. Work may be filigreed, having the background cut out and replaced with a leather of a contrasting color. Or a piece may be made to stand out by pressing out from behind and permanently filling the cavity with kapok or other fiber filler. Glue it in and line with leather or fabric. For a very complete rundown on tooling, I recommend Klingsmith's *Leatherwork Procedure and Design* (see Bibliography).

Another technique which uses many of the same skills as tooling is *molding*. In fact, these two techniques are often used in conjunction, as on the suitcase in Figure 3-6. We've seen that tooling is done on nearly dry, mellow leather. But you should never punch holes in any but dry leather; for it is extremely flexible in the damp state and if bent or pulled when wet, it will stay bent when dry. As you can imagine, wet leather is excellent for molding.

Molding enables you to create many shapes which are impossible to develop any other way. The suitcase mentioned above will be used as an example of the versatility of molded leather. Note the 1½-inch border around the front flap pocket. This was not cut in its present "C" shape but was molded from a straight piece. It was measured, as were the

Figure 3-5 A 2 to 3-ounce vegetable-tanned cowhide billfold, showing a contemporary approach to tooling. Hand painted with aniline dyes. (Courtesy of The Stitching Horse, New York City)

61

holes, cased, sewn and hammered into place. It was then weighted while drying.

Ron Kwiatkowski's superb leather bottle, shown in Figure 1-8 was formed by casing, stretching and nailing it over a wooden form. It was then tooled, using modeling and carving. Allowed to dry completely, it retained its shape.

ASSEMBLING

Now that the pieces have been painstakingly designed, cut and finished, the immediate impulse is to put them together to see what your work has amounted to. But before you hastily knock together whatever you've been making, remember all your planning and work and remember that this very last stage can make a big difference. Not only is stitching noticeable (favorably or otherwise), but a good pattern doesn't amount to anything if you put it together wrong. Also, if you have made a drastic error and let it go this long, you can usually salvage it here.

Figure 3-6 A 4 to 5-ounce vegetable-tanned cowhide suitcase with a front flap and an enclosed pocket. The form was molded, and saddle stitched with waxed linen thread. Modeled designs of various animals cover the bag. By the author.

There are at least four ways to put together leather goods: handsewing with thread, machine sewing, thonging and lacing. Each method holds pieces of leather together, consists of strands going through holes and should (and can) look very good.

To handsew, your basic needs are a needle, thread and a punch. (A spacing wheel is nice but often not necessary or practical.) Punch holes first. Any number between two and sixty to the inch is fine. (Normally two to four is best.) Ideally, use a six or eleven-strand waxed linen thread in heavier leathers and thinner linen or silk in light leather. The linen is strong and the wax helps it hold. Estimate how much thread you will need by simply laying the thread around the perimeter of the parts to be stitched. Then add 6 to 8 inches for knots, and more if you plan a complex stitch. Minimize knots; the more knots, the weaker the seam. To start, loosely knot the end and sew from the inside through the second hole. Go through the first hole twice to reinforce it. There are several types of stitches, including the lock stitch, saddle stitch, single and double running stitch, and back stitch (see Figure 3-7).

The *saddle stitch* is the strongest for heavier work, while almost any of the others will work well in garment leather. Two needles are passed through one hole at the same time and stitches may be drawn very tight. I prefer to use the *double running stitch,* for I've found it easier to handle only one needle. Also, it is nearly as strong, looks the same and the first time around holds the leather in place for the second stitch, when you really draw it down. Ornaments, beads, feathers or fringe may be sewn wherever it suits you.

The awl (or fid) is a great aid to the handsewer. If you ever get in a tight spot and can't seem to get the needle through, force the hole open with the scratch awl's tapered shaft. Another good sewing trick: when sewing a bag closed and you can't find the hole on the inside, insert the awl from the outside, match points, withdraw the awl and bring the needle through.

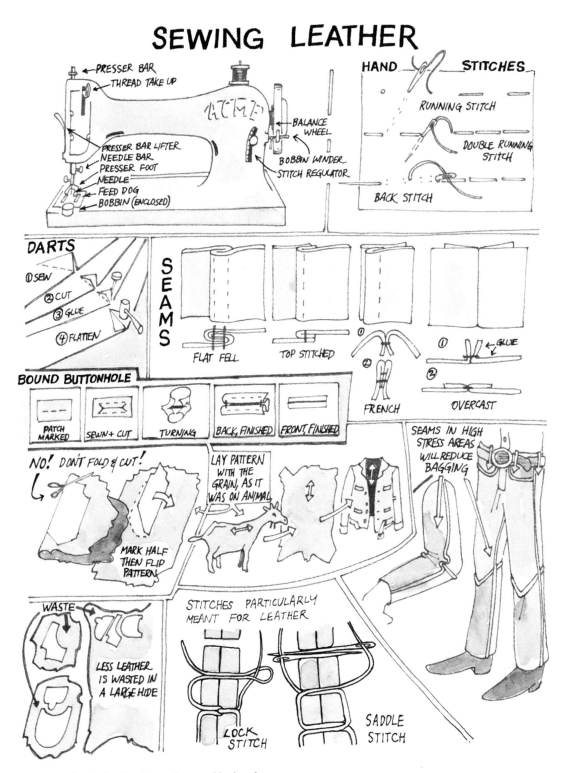

Figure 3-7 Sewing leather by machine and by hand.

Machine sewing lacks the handmade look, obviously, but in sewing clothing it is much faster than hand methods (see Chapter 5, "Clothing"). The actual machine sewing is handled in leather much as it is in fabric. The same seams are taken and the principles for fitting are the same. The machine should have, however, a rolling or walking presser foot. Leather will bind in the machine if a normal presser foot is used. The manual for the machine or a dealer may help you locate such a foot for your machine.

Thonging is the sewing together of a leather article with a ¼-inch thong cut from the same leather or from a contrasting leather. Thongs may also be bought, but are relatively expensive when pre-cut. Here, as in handsewing, several patterns are possible (see Figure 3-8).

The splicing of two thongs in the middle of a piece can be troublesome. There are several ways of splicing thongs (see Figure 3-9). As previously mentioned, a thonged article must have an even number of holes to run the thong through, or it will start on one side (inside) and end on the other (outside). I find thonging to be a durable, attractive, unusual way to assemble leather goods. Depending on its application, it can look rustic or quite polished.

Lacing is an extremely decorative type of thonging, using a commercial leather lace or, more often, plastic stripping. Leather edge lacing is often used to good advantage with tooled leathers. They are a good combination, one complementing the other. There are several excellent texts devoted solely to tooling and lacing and I refer the reader to these.

One last point about assembly—the order of assembly itself. It has been seen that a piece which is to be dyed should by all means be dyed before assembly to assure an even coating. The seams, buckles and holes keep the dye from spreading evenly. The same is true of assembly. It is often *much* easier to sew on a handle when the piece is flat and one-dimensional than to wait until the piece is nearly done, when you must reach inside and grope blindly. The same is

true with pockets, straps and tabs. Flat, you can measure and be sure your work is accurate. Assembled, you take a chance of having a crooked whatever. But I almost always wait to attach the parts which logically should have been attached earlier. Somehow, I want to see that piece near completion and I must figure out exactly what will complete the design. You know it needs a closure, but what kind? How long a strap? A one-dimensional drawing can help you plan your article, but often you must actually see and hold it to complete it effectively.

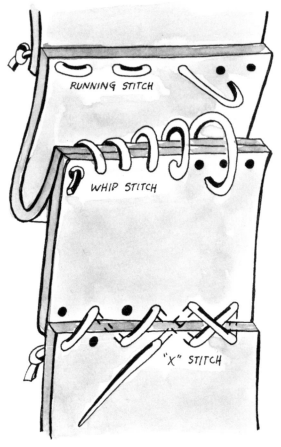

Figure 3-8 A few of many possible hand thonging stitches.

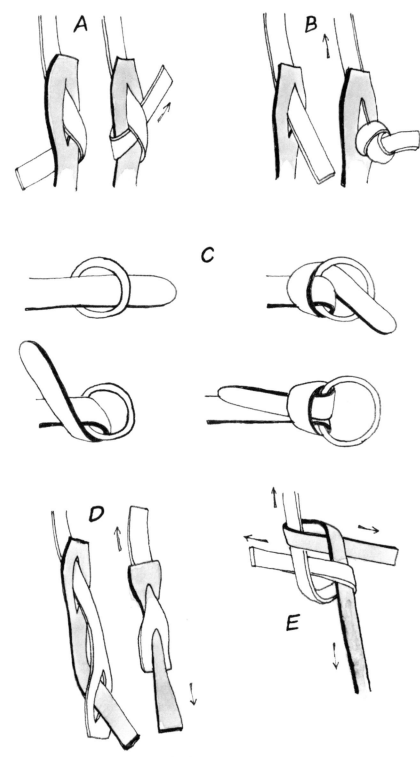

Figure 3-9 Five very neat ways to splice or knot leather.

In Case of Error

A large amount of leatherwork is created with spontaneity and the nature of the material plays a major role. Leather's experimental use has resulted in many new and interesting applications. Freshness, however, is no excuse for a lack of craftsmanship, which is the ability to produce and the actual production of articles whose material is completely understood and used well.

A craftsman's ability requires this intimacy and is not determined by the amount of time spent or by the degree of sophistication. There are times in the production of crafts, though, when there's a slip of the knife or a miscalculation and alterations become necessary. Here are some ideas on how to avoid, repair or revise some errors which you may make in leatherwork. The challenge is to create and this section will help you do that by learning how to get out of sticky situations.

The typical production procedures detailed above are again referred to here with slight alterations. Common problems are mentioned and possible solutions are stated.

DESIGNING THE ITEM
One major problem is that a design simply may not work—physically or aesthetically. The only cure here is to redefine the elements and properties of the proposed article, then either redesign parts or the whole. Make lots of sketches. Better now than after the leather is cut.

DEVELOPING THE PATTERN
Carelessness holds things up here and the only cure is prevention. Be precious with your pattern and with careful measurement and drawing of the actual working model of your design. Be sure of all lines and what they represent. Here, as in designing, an untrue pattern is best done over.

BUYING THE LEATHER
A mistake here means you've bought too little or the wrong kind of leather. If you don't have enough to finish a piece and can't get more of the exact leather, contrast it with another of different weight, color or texture; or insert another material, like wood or handwoven fabric. Remember that an "almost match" is the worst match. If you've purchased the wrong type of leather, either store it for later use, design a new article or adapt the leather to what you have planned. For example, two layers of a thin leather can be used as would a thicker hide.

LAYING OUT THE PATTERN
In the laying out of patterns on the actual leather, care must be taken; mistakes are generally not apparent until after the leather is cut. Watch out for unevenness of any kind—wrinkles, color, creases, holes, weak spots and edges which may be spongy. You needn't discard or even avoid these irregularities, but be aware of them and make them work to your advantage. For example, an article made of heavily creased shoulder leather would look strange if the creases ran diagonally. Lay out the pattern so they complement the overall design, running either horizontally or vertically.

Another consideration when laying out the pattern is the leather which will be left over. Try to get as much out of the hide as possible by butting straight edges and arranging pieces closely. Try to fit a pattern piece in a place into which no other piece would fit. Keep the hide whole when possible, as this reduces scrap. Try to plan room for future pattern pieces.

CUTTING AND TRIMMING TO SIZE
Problems here are of the most frustrating sort, because they are so obvious afterwards and could have been avoided. A miscalculated pattern resulting in a mis-cut piece should

Kangaroo leather, the strongest known, was used in this "Mosque Appliqué Folio." Brightly colored appliqués create a mirror-imaged design. By Ben Liberty. (Photograph by James Utter)

Sandal-shoes, made of cowhide sole leather and blue pigskin uppers, have molded arches and several lifts in the heels. By Ben Liberty. (Photograph by Jeff Boxer)

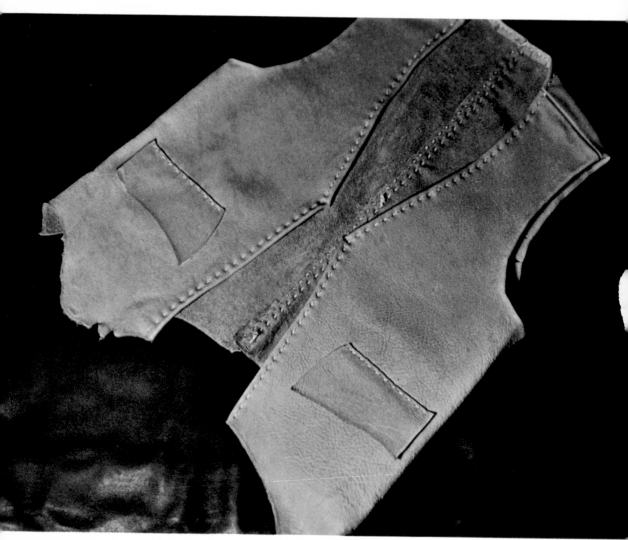

A hand thonged, natural color garment leather vest. A casual nature is developed in the seams and uncut edges of the pockets and the vest itself. By Pat Chobot. (Courtesy of Jim Martin)

have been corrected earlier. There is, however, a cure for nearly every cutting mistake, even crooked cuts and straps cut too short.

The theory behind repairing a mistake, especially when the leather is cut wrong, is to devise some sort of insert or fancy detail which fits the intended space or covers a spoiled spot. Don't try to perfectly repair a mistake in cutting—the repair will show and will look mediocre. Rather, let an accident open your imagination. A too-short strap can be spliced, a ring may be inserted or the buckle can be put on an added tab to give the needed length. Edge-bevel and crease a crooked cut. A piece that's too big can be cut down and a piece that's too small can be joined with another. Preserve the design integrity of the piece and the mistake will work in your favor.

EDGING

This practice presents no problem in any leather. Vegetable-tanned leather takes a crease best, especially if the leather is cased and the creaser is heated first. Leathers thinner than 3-ounce are not usually edged.

DYEING AND FINISHING

Read labels, follow instructions and allow enough time for drying between coats and you should have no problems. Always test dyes and finishes on an inconspicuous part of the object or on a scrap of the same leather. Apply all dyes and finishes evenly and rapidly to avoid streaking. Some leathers dye better damp. Always dye light to dark; that is, apply lighter colors before darker ones. If streaking should occur, or if the color is not pleasing, apply additional coats to cover what you don't like. Always apply a wax finish to prevent fading.

TOOLING AND SURFACE EMBELLISHING

Be sure to use vegetable-tanned leather. Test all leathers before beginning, because some should be dyed before tooling and others after. Case the stock and keep a sponge and water handy for re-wetting. Burnish out all mistakes with a burnisher or a spoon. Back all embossed parts which exceed ⅛ inch in height with leather forms or kapok filler. You may wish to finish a tooled piece with an antiquing finish which highlights the modeling.

ASSEMBLING

If your pieces don't fit together, you'll have to cut and fit an insert, as mentioned above. The actual assembly, though, may sometimes cause problems. If you're sewing on a machine and can't handle it, or can't reach places, you can sew an almost identical stitch by hand.

Handsewing with waxed linen thread is generally no problem, if the holes match. Sewing tricks have already been mentioned, such as the use of the harness awl to cut holes, the scratch awl to assure evenness of holes and to open holes wider and needle-nose pliers to pull needles and thongs out of tight spots. A very nice stitch which is nearly as tight as, and much easier to perform than, the saddle stitch is the double running stitch.

Lacing or thonging can get very confusing, especially if you are lacing pockets into the seam and need to go through as many as four layers with each stitch. Slippage of pieces can be reduced by tacking with rubber cement. Each lacing pattern is done with a series of identical stitches, so master one and they'll all be easy. Practice on a very small sample, which is not as heavy, cumbersome or confusing.

Never discard a piece of leather because of an error. Save it, if only for use as scrap, or if only to help you remember and learn from your mistake. Better yet, let those mistakes pull you out of a designing rut by making your imagination work. Develop enough skill and facility with your materials, that is, enough craftsmanship, so that you can execute any new idea in any direction.

69

Quality in Production and Design

Quality is that factor which will determine your standing as a craftsman; it will give you the option of using or selling your goods, or deny you the possibility of being able to *give* them away.

Well-made goods are a harmonious union of ideas, design, materials and construction. A leatherworker I know designs very fine and unusual purses; but all too often I've seen her use leather which is much too lightweight for the purpose. The result is an abortive attempt at craftsmanship. Even more often I've seen leatherworkers use the very finest leather of just the right weight and tannage but botch the job completely because of faulty and/or careless construction procedures.

A true craftsman is able to employ each tool and leather in the most advantageous manner. He has learned this skill, usually the hard way, through endless experimentation. And that's what I'm recommending to the reader.

The following is excerpted from the "Quality Guidelines of Jefferson County Crafts," a crafts training and marketing program designed to revive the old-time handcrafts in Jefferson County, New York. These guidelines were developed to apply to many crafts and suit our purposes quite well. Ask yourself these questions regarding your goods:

1. Does the item serve a function and fill a need? The craft field in general is sometimes given a poor reputation by those who make easy, "frilly" type things which are just "pretty" and merely decorative. This is not to say that all crafts *must* be purely functional, but only that the design of the whole should make a unique contribution to its function.

2. Is it well made? This almost goes without saying and can only be answered by the careful craftsman. It may mean, in one case, that your stitches are straight and, in another, that your pieces are properly put together.

3. Are the materials used in good taste? Remember the old adage, "You can't make a silk purse out of a sow's ear"? You needn't be using the most expensive materials on the market, but use good quality materials throughout. Avoid gaudy or careless use of materials.

4. Does the item have a handmade quality? Note that "handmade" does not mean sloppily made, but intricately, carefully made. You can do things with your hands that no machine can duplicate.

5. Price: Are you asking too much or too little? (If you are selling goods see the Appendix.) Be fair to everyone—yourself, the retailer and the consumer. Your "labor of love" may appear overpriced to an "outsider." But don't undersell yourself, either.

We have seen that there is a practically endless variety of tools and leathers available. Experiment with leathers and tools to know how to apply each. Learn to work neatly, tastefully and effectively. You will learn only by doing. Consider the design while you experiment and work. The design of any item is a very personal decision, but since the design determines what the item is, it should be a well thought-out, mature decision without the loss of valuable spontaneity. Ironically, the creativity and freshness which are replaced by calculating knowledge become more valuable to the artisan (and sometimes harder to arrive at) as his skill increases. The design should be functional before it is decorative, but with a flair. For example, institutional dishes are extremely functional, but there's nothing more boring to eat off every day. Fine china is beautiful, but I'd hate to have it in my charge to keep a set in one piece. The dish I would buy is handsome, yet durable.

When you design a piece, it should be unique, functional and well-made. Show imagination in your designs; do variations on a theme rather than repeating the same hackneyed designs. Determine what elements exist in a piece and use a little originality to make them unique. By varying or emphasizing one or another of these elements, you will be developing your design sensibilities.

Secondary design deals with integrating and coordinating the elements of a piece. If a bag is laced with thongs, you wouldn't want to stitch the handle on with linen thread. If you have all brass rivets, you will need a brass finding closure. A bag which is round will call for round, not square, pockets. Secondary design strengthens, through unity, the primary design of the piece.

Most leather goods have some metal in the form of rivets, rings and buckles or other findings. Choose a metal which coordinates well with your leather. Copper, silver and brass are exceptionally good. Avoid plated findings, for the plating always wears off and looks very bad. I prefer solid brass findings. They are heavy, never wear out and their color is particularly pleasing, becoming nicer with age. You can make your own findings from brazing rod, ceramics or wood. Don't stick only to buckles. There are literally hundreds of feasible designs for findings which you can use: plugs, rings and weights in the form of stars, moons, circles, ovals, squares.

There are many findings manufacturers (see List of Suppliers) who would love to send you a catalog. But there are other sources for the more imaginative findings. Check a boat supply shop or marina; ships' findings, normally brass, are extremely unusual. Look into a saddle or harness shop for old buckles or harness findings. Your effort will be worth it, for the findings can often make a crucial difference in a piece.

Try collecting bits and pieces of metal which you can work into buckles and other findings. Brass, copper, zinc—even pewter, silver (see Figure 4-19) and gold—work very well. Iron and steel are common and often you can find pieces in interesting shapes. Given a coat of clear lacquer, they will not rust.

Constantly challenge and refine your ideas. Use as many techniques in as many different ways as you can. Never become complacent or stagnant with one approach. Remember: quality craftsmanship equals knowledgeable use of tools, materials and design.

Chapter 4
Leather Accessories

Belts

Belts, wide or narrow, plain or fancy, are a natural for the leathercrafter. They are good for beginners as well as advanced craftsmen because they can be completed relatively rapidly and because a great deal of variation is possible within the restrictions inherent in an article whose physical function is (supposed to be) to hold up your drawers.

We, as humans, don't like to stick to bare necessities; we like variation, such as fringe, intricate or strong, basic designs. And here the leatherworker has an interesting challenge: to make an article that looks very handsome and fills the requirements for which it was originally designed.

When making leather goods, your choice of leather depends on the qualities you're looking for. For belts, those qualities are strength, durability, thickness and resistance to stretch. The best leather for belts would be 7 to 8-ounce vegetable or combination-tanned cowhide. Of the several cuts of leather you can buy, the shoulder is probably the most economical, because there is less waste. The shoulder is cut nearly rectangular with straight sides and averages 12-square feet. Strap after strap can be cut and the piece can be used with minimum waste. A side of leather is a good choice too; but start from the backbone and work toward the belly, realizing that the further down the hide you work, the poorer the leather.

Because of its simple shape, you don't really need a pattern for a belt. Instead, cut the backbone or the longest side of your hide perfectly straight and take special care to keep your next cut very accurate, since one crooked cut will ruin two successive straps. This is where your draw gauge is especially effective. However, a carefully handled mat knife gives equally good results.

Whatever width you cut your straps, they must be of the proper size for the buckle you plan to use. Make sure the belt is not too wide to go through your pant loops. Using a scrap of paper, measure and mark the width of the bar, the part which attaches to the belt (see Figure 4-3). It is better to have this measure a bit on the narrow side, since the belt will be easier to fasten and will look better if the belt end slides through the buckle easily.

Like shoes, sandals and hats, a belt will hurt or annoy the user if it is just a bit too big or small. How do you determine size? It is easiest to start with a belt for yourself, since you can always take your measurement. If you can't fit it to the person, there's only one thing to do: read on.

Belts are sized in even numbers: 28, 30, 32, 34, 36, most having five holes for adjustability. A belt is sized from where the tongue or stud engages with the middle hole (see Figure 4-4). This mid-hole is, as a rule of thumb, 4 inches from the end of the belt, with the other four holes one inch apart. You can make a template, or a pattern for punching, which will work on 99 percent of your belts.

As for the buckle end, you will need at least 2 inches to fold over to attach the buckle. There is a belt feature called a keeper, a simple leather ring which keeps the end of the belt from flapping. Some buckles don't need keepers; but if you are using one, you will need at least 3 inches to

fold over (see Figure 4-5). The keeper is riveted or sewn under the fold, which keeps it in place. An L-shaped piece of leather can be riveted into a ring with a tab, which you can fasten to a 2-inch or less fold. This method, however, is not as strong or effective as the aforementioned.

You can compute the length strap needed for a given waist by adding 6 to 7 inches to the waist measure—4 inches at the hole end and 2 to 3 inches at the buckle end. For example, a belt which is to fit a 32-inch waist should be made from a 38-inch blank.

The belt ends should be rounded to give a stronger design. A square end stops the eye and shows a lack of imagination and/or skill, while a curved end flows. Besides, a rounded end goes through the buckle more easily. Belt end rounding or tapering is accomplished in one of two ways. You can buy a belt end punch (built like an arch punch) which, with one good swat, gives you a perfect end every time. Or you can cut the ends by hand, as I always do, with very good re-

Figure 4-1 A Navajo Indian belt, ca. 1900, from the collection of Mrs. Margaret W. M. Shaeffer. The conchos are solid silver and the strap is 7 to 8-ounce oiled cowhide.

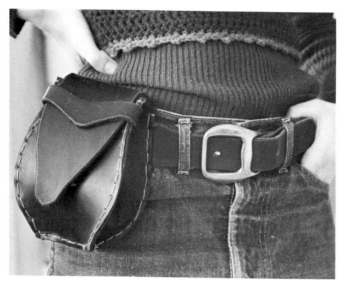

Figure 4-2 A belt of 6 to 7-ounce hand-dyed yellow latigo. The removable pouch, which expands to about twice the size shown, is of the same leather. Both are sewn with linen thread. By the author.

sults. To hand cut a belt end, first square the end at the correct length. Then cut the corners off at 45°, keeping the two sides even. Then cut off these corners. This curve will be slightly bumpy, but by the time the belt is edge-beveled, dyed, saddle soaped and creased, it will be smooth enough to look neat and rough enough to look handmade. Complete the curve (rounded or pointed) with these six cuts. Don't try to round the ends with curved cuts because your knife will drag; and more likely than not, the curve will be uneven (see Figure 4-6).

Edging and dyeing proceed as normal; punching the holes to fit the buckle has only a slight modification. Fold the belt end over as it will go when the buckle is attached and mark the midpoint of this fold. Here you will punch a hole to accept the tongue on your buckle. Use a bag punch to allow room for the hinge which holds the tongue to the bar. A stud tongue buckle will have no hole in this fold. With a scratch awl, mark where your rivets will go. You want them close enough to the buckle to hold it securely, but not so close that it binds. On a 2-inch fold,

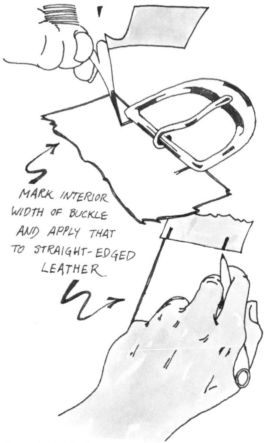

MARK INTERIOR WIDTH OF BUCKLE AND APPLY THAT TO STRAIGHT-EDGED LEATHER

Figure 4-3 Mark the width of the buckle to make a properly sized belt blank.

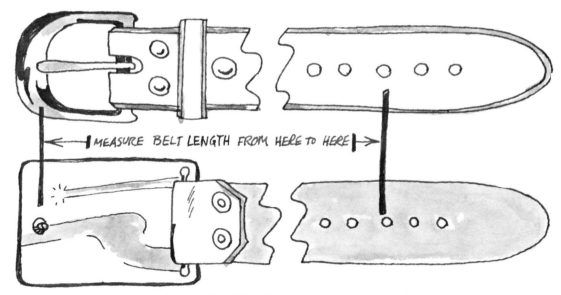

Figure 4-4 Measure properly to be sure the belt fits the intended wearer.

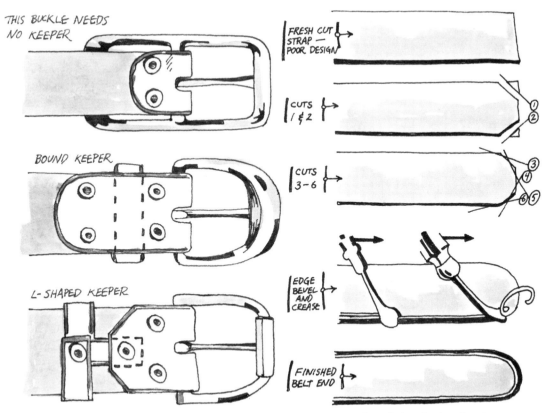

Figure 4-5   Belt keepers, back view, showing the attachment of buckles.

Figure 4-6 Rounding a belt end using six cuts.

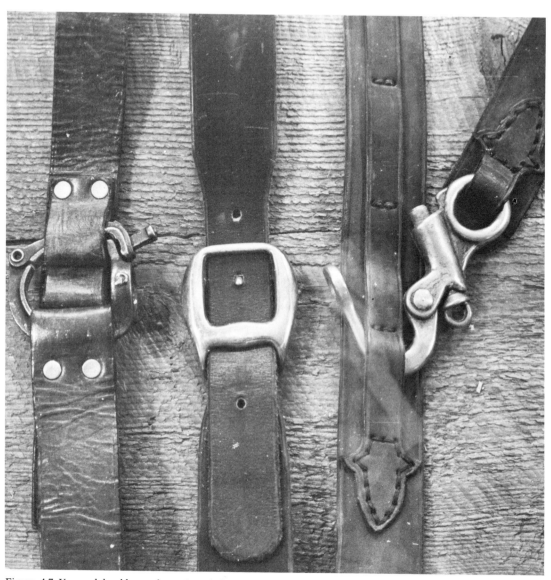

Figure 4-7 Unusual buckles make unique belts. From the left, the buckles are: a steel fitting, which normally holds a water pipe to a wall; an antique brass horse harness buckle (note the tapering of the belt); a ship's brass fitting. By the author.

two or three rivets are good; on a 3-inch fold, use three or four. Punch the marked holes out, skive for easy folding, fold and mark through with the awl. Punch these, insert and set your rivets and drive them home.

When working in a small space such as between the keeper and the buckle, it may be difficult or impossible to hit the rivets without marring or possibly tearing the leather. Here's a helpful trick: use a small piece of steel to hold the rivet in the belt and on an anvil. Strike that steel with your hammer and the rivet will be fastened without leaving a mark. Here's another helpful hint. In making a belt keeper, a ring of leather is riveted

together; here again you may damage your leather with hammer marks. Again insert a small piece of steel in the ring, using it as your anvil and saving your leather's face.

Apply a coat or two of saddle soap and you're done. After all my explanations and all your work and experimentation, we now can see that a belt really always was and always will be just something to hold up your pants. How can we make it something more?

The buckle is the focal point and determines how the belt is constructed and fastened. By using unusual buckles, you can make your belts unique. Commercial buckle companies are making noble attempts at

Figure 4-8 (a) A selection of fine tooled belt blanks of 5-ounce oak-tanned cowhide. By John Coutoupis; (b) A very decorative style with patterns of rivets and bright dye. By Robin Lorenz.

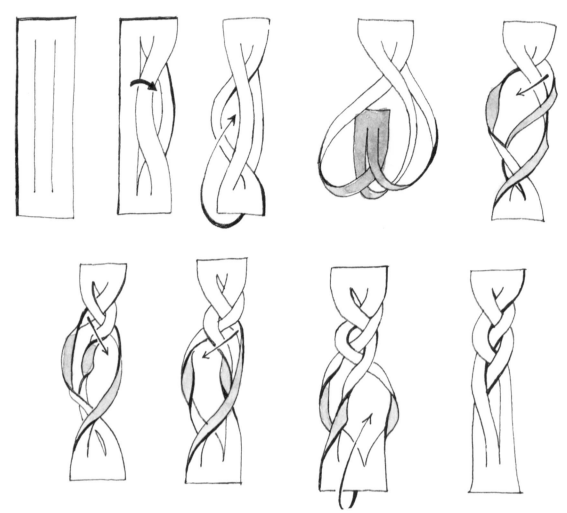

Figure 4-9 The trick braid (with as many as eight parts) enables you to braid a strap without cutting open either end. Carefully follow the drawings, keeping the braid as tight as possible. When you can go no further, spread the braid out evenly over the length.

manufacturing unique buckles. Brass buckles can now be bought in a spectrum of fancy designs. Still and all, these buckles are commercial and every "unique" finding has 10,000 twin brothers. I enjoy seeking out odd bits of hardware, the actual function of which I usually don't know, and using them as findings, particularly belt buckles. For the most part, these "buckles" have neither tongues nor studs, so new ways of fastening and adjusting them must be designed.

Another way of making your belts unique is to work with the leather in unusual ways. Tooling or the trick braid are effective embellishments for belts. The appearance is worth the time they take. Or you can make a design running the length of the belt using incised lines, dye or rivets, in any combination.

78

Bags

Strength, durability and flexibility make leather an excellent material for the production of all types of satchels. Carrying cases made of leather are found everywhere and there are hundreds of different types and sizes of cases. Hand-held bags, for men and women, may be of nearly any size, from a suitcase to a briefcase to a handbag. Any shape may be developed and nearly any leather may be used. Besides being hand-held, they may also have a shoulder strap or a handle which converts to a shoulder strap. There are as many ways of putting a bag together as there are of getting it to stay shut once it is assembled. Many complementary materials including brass, bone, ivory, wood, shells and feathers may be used to enhance a bag's appearance.

Bags can have several compartments, can have pockets including secret ones, can hang

Figure 4-10 Saddlebags of 6 to 7-ounce yellow latigo. By the author.

Figure 4-11 A unique knapsack: the flap is of 7 to 8-ounce latigo, and the bag is of reversible garment leather. By Barry Olen. (Photograph by Don Rosen)

79

open or have a flap, can be dark or light, rough or smooth. All bags must be designed to conveniently carry and protect articles and must be attractive, functional and easy to fasten securely.

Bags can be made of nearly any type or weight leather, depending on the qualities desired. If the leather is any thinner than 4-ounces, it will be a limp bag, but one into which many things may be stuffed. If the leather is thicker than 6-ounces, it will weigh quite a bit no matter what the size. Also, the walls will not bend much, thus restricting the size and shape of the articles carried. Generally, heavier leathers are used in cases which are made for carrying a specific item; the case is fitted to the object.

A good, very adaptable leather which may be used in many ways is 4 to 6-ounce cowhide, preferably vegetable tanned. It can be tooled, molded, turned inside out, dyed or have piping sewn in. It can be sewn by a

Figure 4-12 A 3 to 4-ounce sueded leather bag is supple and flexible. A pattern of leather strips of a contrasting color has been woven into the flap. (Courtesy of The Stitching Horse, New York City)

Figure 4-14 A freely made, intricately beaded, hand thonged bag. Silver, bone and leather braid has also been added. Three-ounce chrome-tanned waxed cowhide of russet color. By Eugenie Berman.

80

Figure 4-13 A superior leather box of goat hair skin, off-set by finished, heavy stock and brass corners. By Scott Nelles. (Photograph by the artist)

heavy-duty machine or by hand, or it can be laced, all with excellent results. Obtainable in shoulders and sides, dyed or completely unfinished, it is not too expensive for the novice and gives excellent results. It is light enough to be quite flexible and heavy enough to hold its shape. From this starting point, you will soon see whether you wish to use heavier, lighter or same stock leather.

The elements of a bag are the strap, sides, flap, closure or latch, front and back, whatever pockets are used and the stitching or lacing. Combine these elements in their common interpretations and you have an ordinary bag which may be very functional but not very exciting. Try to find new ways to interpret these elements and incorporate them in your work. As soon as you alter one element—for example, changing a buckle closure to a brass ring, or a polished stone—you get a bag which is a bit out of the ordinary. Change two or three elements and you have a bag which is uniquely your own. Be wary, though, of too much diversity. A bag, being a unit, must have some unifying factors, such as similar curves or lacing or tooling of the same designs throughout.

The purpose of a *strap* is for carrying the bag; it can be made adjustable in any of several ways, changing its function (and affect-

81

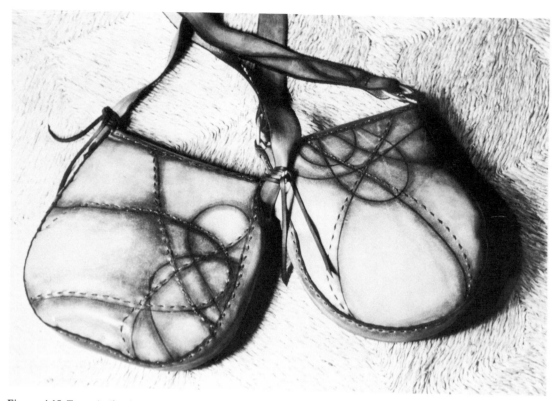

Figure 4-15 Two similar but uniquely different hand-bags. By Pat Chobot. (Courtesy of Jim Martin)

ing its originality) from a hand strap to shoulder or across-the-body strap. You can insert a buckle, attach a clip, or make your strap fully adjustable by using holes and thongs (see Figure 4-17).

The *sides or gusset(s)* are of two types and there are two basic variations of these. One type of gusset runs completely around a bag, from one corner to the other, comprising both sides and the bottom. It may also continue up into the strap, or the strap and gusset may all be one piece. This is called a *continuous gusset*. The second type is called the *patch gusset* and is made of two separate pieces of leather which close the sides (or

ends) of a bag. A patch gusset is used when a single piece of leather makes up the front, bottom and back (and even top and flap) of a bag. Both the continuous and the patch gussets may be cut in different manners. One variation is the *straight gusset*, or one which is of an equal width all over. The other is the *expanded gusset*. This variation gets wider at the bottom, giving the bag a more contoured look and more interior space (see Figure 4-18). Your bags can have a *straight continuous* or *straight patch gusset;* or they may have an *expanded patch* or *expanded continuous gusset*.

The *flap* is the major focal point of a bag. The strength of the design of the flap is very

82

important, yet it should not overpower or contradict the body of the bag. You are dealing mainly with one-dimensional designs applied to the flap, that is, tooling or decorative stitching, and with the one-dimensional design of the cut lower edge—in contrast to the three-dimensional design of the rest of the bag. This design can reflect the design of the rest of the bag, having the same curves or straight lines. It can be round-cornered and symmetrical, for symmetry always gives design strength and safety; or the flap (or the whole bag for that matter) can be cut asymmetrically in a flowing design. Another interesting way of imparting a vibrant quality to your bag is to use a natural uncut edge of leather as the outline of the flap (see Figure 4-20). A bag does not necessarily need a flap. It can be made to close without one or it may hang open. Without a flap however, you lose the option of incorporating a strong, functioning, one-dimensional design in your three-dimensional work.

The *closure or latch* on a bag is similar to that on a belt: it holds the article closed, should be easy to use and is the main non-leather element. The design problems (and possibilities) are compounded in a bag, however, since the flap and latch must work together, both physically and in a design sense. While the flap is the focal point of the bag, the latch is the focal point of the flap; and they must complement each other. Belt buckles are often used as bag closures, as are rings, bone, wood or ceramic (see Figure 2-7). Here again, it is important, for both design and originality, to have some unique hardware as closures. Simple or fancy, the best latches are those which are one-of-a-kind, easy to use, pleasing to the eye, complementary to the design of the bag and noncorroding.

There are other possibilities, though, besides metal findings. Closing a leather bag with leather is not only consistent in a design sense, but gives you the opportunity to stretch your imagination and to exercise originality. It's also less expensive than buying metal findings and the effect can be

Figure 4-16 A man's goatskin bag, brightly colored and hung with fringe. Touareges leatherwork, Arabia. (Courtesy of Dan Pejovic)

equally good or better. I'd recommend that if you can't afford *quality* metal findings, use leather closures (see Figure 4-22). Remember that the purpose of any latch is to hold the bag securely shut—until you want it open, at which point it should disengage easily. While you may lose shiny, heavy metal fasteners, leather closures are built right into a bag, being totally unified in every way.

Pockets are a convenience item and because of the difficulty in attaching them, some people don't feel they are necessary. But I've heard it said that a bag with no pockets is like using a paper sack. Pockets on the outside can be sewn in with the rest of the bag, or they can be appliquéd. They

83

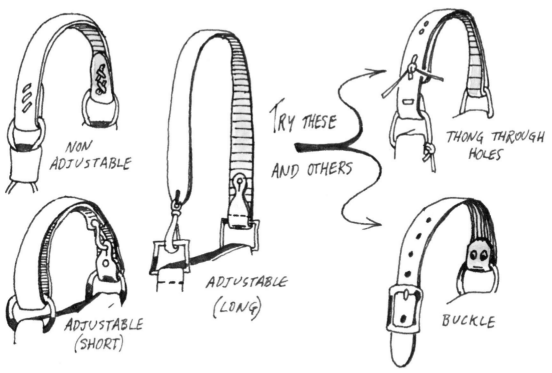

Figure 4-17 Different types of straps.

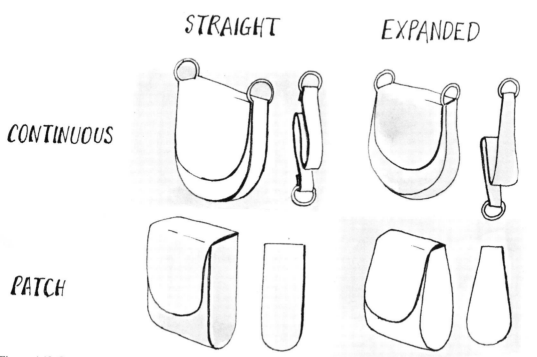

Figure 4-18 Gussets, or side pieces, are of several designs for several types of bags.

can be simply a single piece, or can be expandable with a gusset of their own. They can be set on the flap (possibly making it heavy enough to dispense with a finding closure), back, front or gusset of a bag. Inside pockets can be made identically like outside pockets; or they can be made like most pants pockets—a free-hanging pouch attached only at the rim. A bag can be given two interior compartments by using one "partition" of leather. I once made a purse with two secret compartments. Two small interior flaps lifted to reveal two slim pockets formed by the space between double walls. Provision can be made for removable pockets (or attachable pockets) inside or out.

Once again, there are many original ways of putting a bag together. Waxed linen

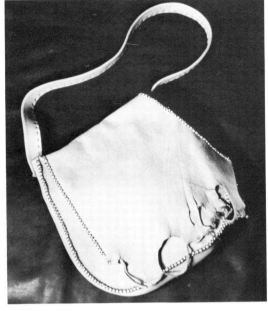

Figure 4-20 The flap of this lightweight leather bag has been tastefully left uncut. By Pat Chobot. (Courtesy of Jim Martin)

Figure 4-19 This design innovation, coupled with turquoise and silver findings, creates a very interesting and unusual bag. By Dan Padilla. (Photograph by L. Paul Robertson)

Figure 4-21 Silver and turquoise as well as fancy lacing grace this bag. The silver medallion is actually attached to the body of the bag and shows through a hole in the flap; an unconventional closure. By Dan Padilla. (Photograph by L. Paul Robertson)

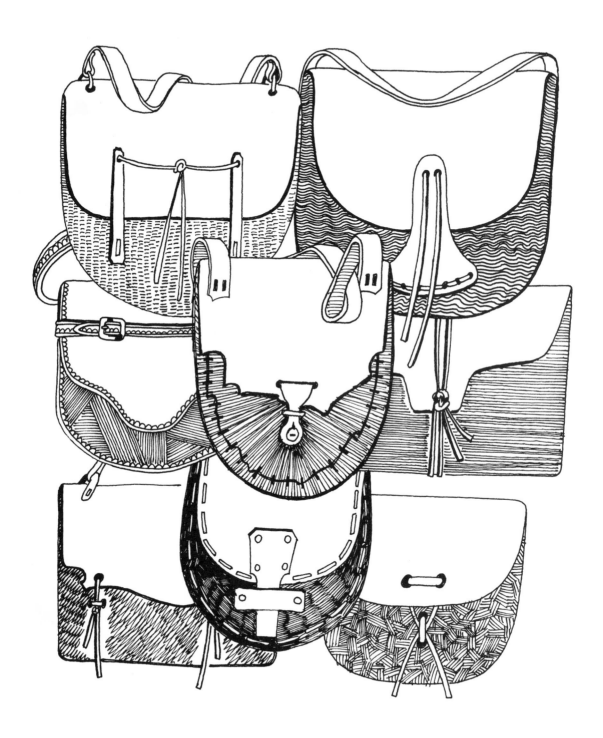

Figure 4-22 Leather closures have many possibilities.

Figure 4-23 A rustic appeal is gained, in part, through the use of leather thongs cut from the same hide. Four to five-ounce waxed-finish Italian cowhide, with handmade brass buckles. By the author.

Hats

thread may be used in a number of different stitches, leather laces may be laced in innumerable ways and leather thongs also have various applications. Machine sewing is an alternative to any of the above. The pieces of a bag could be assembled with rivets or the leather gusset may be replaced by a canvas one. A gusset may be macraméd and tied into the holes punched for lacing.

Just when I thought I had all the methods of leather construction down, I saw a bag which was nailed together with clinching nails and I realized once again that the amount of originality in leatherwork is directly proportional to the number of original leather craftsmen working at any given time.

Hats have always served important physical and psychological functions. Physically, they retain one-tenth of the body heat in winter and shade the wearer in the summer. Psychologically, they make a short person look taller, a good guy look better and enable an early hair-loser to hide that fact. Hats are also an excellent indicator of the wearer's personality. There are literally hundreds of types of hats. You will be able to wear some hats but will feel uncomfortable in others. Choose a design for a hat which you will be able to wear comfortably.

Commercial hats are most often made of felt. Some are made of fabric or fiber glass, as in some women's hats, caps, firemen's hats and helmets. Hats from other eras were made of leather, including the fireman's hat.

87

Figure 4-24 A highly finished, masterly piece done in black cowhide with restraint, taste and a flair for design. By Ben Liberty. (Photograph by Charles Slatkin; courtesy of the artist)

Leather was then recognized as durable, luxurious and an excellent hat material. There is no reason why it can't be so used today.

The leather you choose for hats should be no thicker than 4-ounce. If any thicker, the hat would be too bulky and heavy to wear. The qualities you want in leather for a hat are lightweight, the ability to hold its shape, resistance to waterspotting, an attractive appearance and flexibility. As with handbags, hats are of two basic weights which have a direct relationship to the way they fit: a lightweight suede or garment leather (2 or 3-ounce) will yield a floppy hat, while a leather with more body will give a hat which is correspondingly stiffer. Both approaches can be handled with equally good results; some patterns or types of hats must be made either stiff or floppy, but not both. A bowler or a top hat must be rigid, while a beret must be supple. Some hats combine both rigid and supple leather, like a baseball hat with a soft crown and a rigid brim.

Hats may be sewn by machine or by hand, using heavy mercerized thread or waxed linen. Any of the previously mentioned stitches (such as the lock, saddle or running stitches) can be used to good advantage. Rivets or thongs (again, in any stitch) can be effective. The parts you will assemble are the brim, crown, headband (or sweatband) and hatband (see Figure 4-28). Comfort of the wearer is of primary concern. However you assemble the hat, it must be done so that there is no roughness on the inside to irritate the head. Roughness or crudeness on the outside may or may not irritate the aesthetic senses, depending on the design and feeling of the piece.

Making a pattern for a hat is difficult enough, but when you must make that pattern to fit a certain head it gets very tricky. I advise that you make a pattern from a hat which fits the way you want the new one to. Carefully measure and record the dimensions of the hat. Using these measurements, you now have a basis for developing your own design. Using good sense and these numbers, you can make design variations with a certain amount of assurance that the hat will fit. You can rearrange an existing hat pattern by moving, eliminating or adding

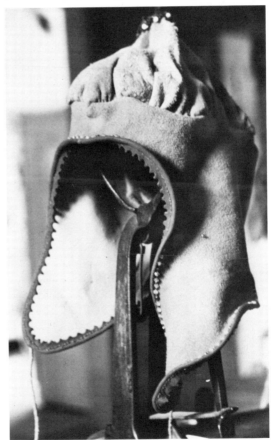

Figure 4-25 "House Bag" of heavy russet leather, hand colored and saddle stitched. A replica of an old style house, complete with shoulder strap (not shown), this is an unusual bag indeed. By Scott Nelles. (Photograph by the artist)

Figure 4-26 An unorthodox hat of lightweight goatskin. By Furry Foote. (Photograph by the artist)

89

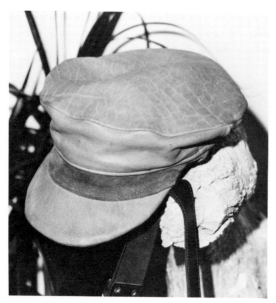

Figure 4-27 The brim and crown are of the same reversible garment leather in this cap. The former is lined to give rigidity while the latter is not. By Barry Olen. (Courtesy of the artist)

seams and pieces. A straight crown can be made to take a rakish angle and a meager brim can be made generous.

Invert the hat and measure the length and width of the opening for the crown. Measure the width of the brim, which may not be the same all the way around. Measure, too, the height of the crown from where it joins the brim to its highest point. Ideally, for most hats, the top of the crown should just brush the top of the head. The brim should run one inch above where the ears join the head, one to two inches above the eyebrow and two inches above where the head joins the neck. If you don't have an old hat to use, measure around the head at these points and across from side to side and from front to back. Also, you must sight the distance from one inch above the ear to the top of the crown and the width and depth in a straight line by holding a ruler and sighting. (See Figure 4-28.) Since these measurements will be something less than scientific, be sure to test them well with a paper pattern. Generally, the crown is about 4 inches tall. The width and

depth of the crown can be worked out between the estimated measures and the circumference of the head. Remember that the head is not round from any view. The top view is almost egg-shaped, longer than wide and narrower at the front.

Develop a drawing and then a pattern of your own design, using the measurements of the head, or preferably the hat. Lay this pattern on newsprint or heavy brown paper, cut it out and make a paper hat. Try it on, tape it well and make adjustments by cutting the paper or adding some on, as needed. This construction of a paper model is an extra step not dealt with earlier. In the long run, it is a time and material saver and is quite necessary when making extremely fitted articles such as hats or garments. Again, as with clothing and sandals, your pattern needs to be the proper size, dimension and design in order to fit well. As with all your leatherwork, the pattern needs to be drawn true, at 90° angles, with an absolute minimum of distortion or miscalculation.

Take your newsprint hat apart carefully and arrange the pieces as closely as possible, in the most advantageous positions, on the flesh side of the skin. Be particularly careful of mars or imperfections in the leather, especially in the brim. This part stands (or flops) on its own strength and needs to be made of good leather. Two or three-ounce leather hats with brims generally need reinforcement in those brims. Three layers of the same light leather, or one light with one slightly heavier leather under it, should give adequate support. Plan to make the crown at least ⅜ inch larger than the paper pattern to allow for the thickness of the leather and the seam. Make the hole in the middle of the brim about this much bigger too, to allow room to attach the crown without binding. Hats use a fair amount of leather, especially if they have large brims. Try to fit a piece, such as the top of the crown, into the hole in the middle of the brim to avoid leather waste.

Cut out and prepare the pieces for assembly, making adjustments as you feel neces-

Figure 4-28 Hats must fit correctly.

sary. Each leather and each hat pattern will require slightly different handling. Take special care with the skiving, as the reduced thickness obtained by this practice is desirable. If you are sewing by hand, punch your holes carefully. Crooked or uneven stitches tend to show up blatantly when you display them on your head. If you are sewing by machine, practice getting your seams straight and be sure to rubber cement both edges to hold them in the proper place for stitching.

Most hats have a separate crown and brim. Normally, the crown is sewn together, then sewn to the brim. Sometimes, however, the crown or even the whole hat may be made of one piece of leather. With the stresses involved, I suggest you limit yourself to a one-piece crown rather than a one-piece hat. Soak vegetable-tanned cowhide until saturated, then stretch and form it by hand, or over a hat block which you may make of pine. The sweatband is sewn or cemented to the inside to minimize the irritation to the head from the seam, and also to absorb sweat. Use a very thin (one to two-ounce) lining leather or a fabric for this. Sometimes a

Figure 4-29 The leather in this hat is sueded on one side and finished on the other. The sueded side is exposed in the crown, which was made inside-out and then turned—a turned crown. In the brim, two pieces of the same leather were laminated, both with finished side out. By Dan Holiday. (Courtesy of the artist)

Figure 4-30 A hat made of 4 to 5-ounce vegetable-tanned cowhide. An X-stitch on the inside gives parallel double stitches on the top of the crown. The others are double running stitches. Note the "sculptured" hatband. By the author.

91

hat will have a turned crown, or one which was assembled inside out then turned right side out to recess the top of the crown and/or to hide the seams in the crown. This practice, however, stresses the leather and the stitches greatly and can be performed only with a very lightweight or very supple skin. It is relatively easy to rip stitches and permanently and unattractively crease the leather while turning a crown. The effect, however, when properly obtained, is very pleasing.

Finish the crown and put the hat together. The brim will automatically take on a pleasant curve which looks good on the head. This curve can be emphasized or exaggerated by soaking and molding. The brim may be sewn to the crown, or the crown to the brim. In other words, the seam may be on the topside or underside of the brim. If it is on the underside, you will need a sweatband. If it is on the topside, your hatband will conceal it. I've seen a very handsome hat in which the hatband fastens crown and brim. Tabs, which are part of the brim, extend into the hole in the brim. These are punched and folded up and a strap is run through them and the crown to hold the whole together.

You may use any system to assemble your hat. I prefer a double running stitch or an "X" stitch. The latter, performed from the inside, yields a motif of parallel double stitches which run perpendicular to the edges of the leather they are sewing. Whatever stitch you use, draw it tight.

The hatband is the "tour de force" in a hat. It is decorative and is a holdover from the days when feathers, ribbons and flowers adorned hats. On a leather hat, a leather hatband makes perfect sense and looks very well indeed. The hatband rests, sometimes unattached, in the junction of crown and brim and should integrate and offset the two. Use leather of a complementary color and texture. Rattlesnake skins are traditional hatbands; and if you have been looking for an appropriate place for your snakeskin, this is it. Don't feel you must limit your hatband to plain leather strips. Develop one which has design and character. In addition to sculptural strips, you can make a very handsome and more conservative hatband by stringing together on a leather strip six or eight shapes or discs of leather. This creates a very effective motif against the crown's leather background, especially if the leathers are of complementary colors. Conchos (metal decorations), shells or beads may be strung; or a hatband may be sewn, woven or macraméd.

Chapter 5
Leather Clothing

Sandals

Sandals consist of simple soles of leather attached to the foot by straps. They are as ancient as they are modern. Records of sandals and sandalmaking have been found in relics from ancient Egypt and Mesopotamia. Every city nowadays has at least one sandal shop catering to the individual desires of its clientele. The making of sandals is one of the most enjoyable endeavors for a leatherworker: a great deal of variation is possible, a pair can be made in two hours and their sale is lucrative, especially if they are custom-made. Sandalmaking is not painstakingly exacting, but a certain amount of precision is necessary. A knowledge of materials as well as imagination and sense of design is needed.

Sandals are worn nearly everywhere. In some climates, they are worn all year long by men, women and children. The number of styles and variations is limited only by the imagination of the sandalmaker and by the anatomy of the foot. Sandals must be neat and must fit well. Any irritation of the feet

Figure 5-1 A selection of sandals in a retail leather goods shop. The customer selects the style and the craftsman custom-makes a pair to fit his foot. By John Watson.

93

cannot be tolerated and is the hallmark of poorly made sandals. To fit a sandal properly, you must understand the foot and know where to put the straps.

The basic parts of the foot (see Figure 5-2) are the toe (or ball) and heel sections, the instep and the arch. These comprise front and back, top and bottom of the foot. Sandals are generally attached to the foot at the toe and instep and sometimes at the heel. Of the several ways to attach the sole at the toe, the two most common are to run a strap around only the large toe and to run a strap covering and holding all five toes without going between any. Other toe attachments include a thong which goes from between the large and second toe to an instep strap, and a button of leather held on a thong which also goes between the large and second toes. Besides being attached at the toe, most sandals are attached at the heel and/or instep. This helps hold the sandal to the foot and gives better support. Straps may be separate from one another; but often an ingenious leatherworker will consider both design and function while developing a pattern that leaves all the straps connected, using only one long strap, which brings a design simplicity and unity and makes the sandal easily adjustable.

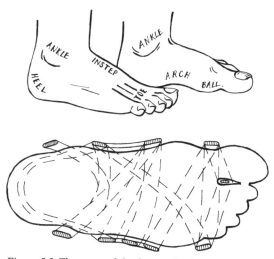

Figure 5-2 The parts of the foot and a few of the many possible strap positions.

Much variation is possible in sandalmaking because straps may cross the foot at any point, in any direction and may join the sole almost anywhere desired, as long as the sole remains comfortably attached to the foot. There are, however, well-tested, comfortable places to run straps and join soles. They are described in the following text and are shown in Figures 5-1 and 5-2.

Behind the large toe but above the bone on the inside of the ball of the foot is the place to run either of the two common toe straps mentioned earlier. The first type goes between the large and second toes (as do the other toe attachments mentioned); while the second would run to just behind the smallest toe, ahead of the bone on the outside of the ball. If the sandal has an instep strap, it goes from the arch on the inside of the foot to the part directly opposite and is angled to fit the slope of the instep. A heel strap should pass below the ankle bones on the inside and outside of the foot; and in back, it should pass over the hamstring for a snug fit.

A professional sandalmaker or shoe repairman has many specific tools for sandalmaking, from sole cutters to burnishing and polishing wheels. While a complete shop is not mandatory for producing sandals, certain supplies and tools are necessary. At least two and normally three different leathers are needed: 10 to 12-ounce sole leather for the lower soles; 4 to 6-ounce vegetable-tanned leather for the straps; and 5 to 7-ounce leather for the upper soles, although the same leather can be used for uppers as for straps. A shoemaker has a solecutter, a hand-cranked machine which cuts heavy leathers; but your mat knife will work well if applied with ample control. Special leather-cutting blades are available for saber saws. A draw gauge is handy but, again, the mat knife suffices. A bag punch is a tool which you really can't substitute. Use it to cut the slots to run the straps through. All-purpose cement and clinching nails are necessary too. A good shoemaker's or square-faced hammer and a steel surface

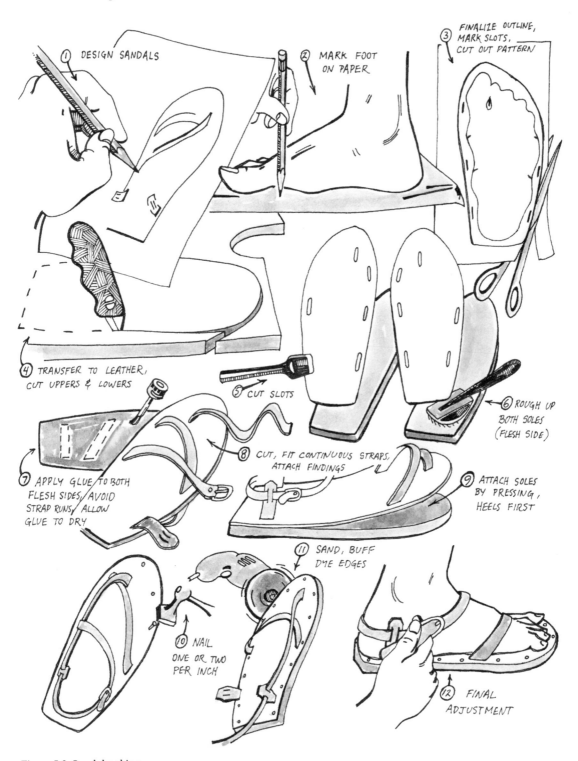

Figure 5-3 Sandalmaking.

are needed, as is a power sander or a drill with a sanding attachment.

After assembling your workshop, you must consider your design. The qualities you should develop in your sandals are good fit, smooth operation and a simple yet effective configuration of straps. These characteristics are interdependent. A good fit means smooth operation and strong design, just as a good design means good fit and smooth operation. As mentioned earlier, try to make all your cross straps from one long piece. It will simplify and strengthen the fit, design and operation. Straps may join the soles as comfort dictates. Avoid places where straps and foot would bind, such as directly on a bone. By changing cross straps, a great variety of designs are feasible. Figures 5-1 and 5-2 give only a few of the many possibilities. Draw out ideas for designs and experiment with different ways of running the straps, whether few or many, parallel to each other or at angles. Keep smoothness of operation in mind.

After you've designed the sandals, have the person for whom you're making them stand barefooted on paper, resting his weight evenly on both feet. Holding a pencil at 90° to the paper, draw completely around the foot. Mark the inside arch (where it leaves and rejoins the paper), the outside of the arch (behind the small bone behind the smallest toe and the bone directly below the anklebone) and the space between the large and second toes. Then measure around the big toe for a single toe strap and across all five toes for that type of toe strap. Always measure the instep; this helps you fit the sandal to the foot by giving an indication of the angle of the instep from ankle to toe. Although you can mark both feet, you really need to mark only the larger foot. Use that one foot pattern flipped over to mark the other sandal. Allowances for size can be made, but it is usually not necessary.

Add ¼ inch all the way around the drawing and even out the outline. You may want to develop a square heel or toe, or round or pointed ones; do this on the pattern. Record your design on the inside of the tracing of the foot. Also mark the places where the straps will run, both cross straps and where they join the soles. Be sure to mark inside the outline. It is discouraging to carefully mark a foot and then lose all your measurements and marks because you've written them outside the pattern line and have discarded the excess after cutting.

Mark and cut your lower soles first. Lay out your pattern on the flesh side of heavy (10 to 12-ounce) sole leather. Draw both feet by flipping the one pattern. Since feet are of similar shape and size, you can intermesh many patterns for feet in a relatively small space. Sole leather is tough and thick; but with several cuts from a very sharp knife, you can do it neatly. Lay out your patterns on the upper leather in the same manner. Put them as close as possible by turning and putting them toe to heel. Cut out the uppers from leather which is preferably 5 to 7-ounce vegetable or chrome-tanned. The upper and lower soles will be put together flesh side to flesh side, giving a finished grain side both top and bottom, with the straps running between them. Cut your straps at the desired width and about 5-feet long from 4 to 5-ounce vegetable-tanned leather. This leather is more mellow to the touch and is less likely to stretch than chrome-tanned leather; these are two important qualities in straps of any type. They should hold the sole comfortably to the foot without binding and should not stretch, for obvious reasons.

Lay out your soles as they will eventually go, left with left, right with right, flesh to flesh. By laying the pattern over the upper and poking with a scratch awl, mark where the strap slots will go and cut them with a bag punch about ¼ inch from the edge. As mentioned in Chapter 2, a small bag punch can make large slots if you run several slots together.

Some sandals have arches, others do not. Some are made with heels and others without. The decision to have arches or heels is a personal one and is up to the designer. There are two types of arches which you may employ, either leather ones or rubber ones. Both are used between the soles. The former are made by the sandalmaker and the latter are purchased. To make your own arches, cut a piece of sole leather the same size as the arch of the foot. If you've made your pattern correctly, this will be marked on it. The arch is the raised space on the inside of the foot. The pattern shows the width and the length is 2 to 3 inches depending on foot size. The height of your arch will be the thickness of your leather, approximately ¼ to ⅜ inch. This piece is skived and goes between the soles to support the arch. Leave the outside edge of the arch the original thickness and gradually skive it paper thin on the interior edge. Rubber arches, called cookies, come in several sizes. Both types are applied in the same manner. They are glued between the soles, then nailed to the lower sole.

There is another type of arch which is equally satisfactory and is made by molding the lower sole. The sole is first cut and cased, then the part which corresponds to the arch of the foot is bent up to fill this hollow. It can be fitted directly to the foot to assure complete fit. At the same time, slightly bend the sole up at the toe and heel for comfort. Allow the sole to dry completely and assemble as usual.

Heels are sometimes applied and are normally of one, two or sometimes three lifts or layers of leather. They are marked with the pattern on scrap sole stock, cut, glued and nailed on. Nail from the lower sole down, that is, with the nail heads between the upper and lower soles, to avoid having nail heads protruding and irritating the foot. Use shoe nails rather than clinching nails. If more than one lift is applied, glue and nail them from bottom to top. If you use three or more lifts, as in a high-heeled sandal, you may find it advantageous to purchase steel shanks, which are inserted between soles to hold the arch in shape. They come in various sizes and may be bought through your shoeman.

On the flesh side of all four soles, draw ink lines connecting the holes where the straps will run. Then rough up all flesh sides with a coarse file and apply all-purpose cement everywhere but where the straps will fall, on both uppers and lowers. This allows free adjustability of the straps. Another way to achieve this is to lay cellophane tape in the places where the straps will go; this acts as a mask or resist and is peeled off after cementing.

Allow the cement to dry completely (sometimes ½ hour) and run the strap(s) through the proper holes in the upper sole. Press the uppers and lowers together, starting at the heel and working forward. Since this is a contact cement, you have only one chance to get the soles together properly. When you have "set" the soles by hand, hammer them together on steel with a shoemaker's hammer to thoroughly set the contact cement. You are now ready to secure the soles together permanently.

There are two methods of permanently affixing the soles and at least two ways to do each. The first system is to *nail* them. Special nails called clinching nails are used, about one per inch. They have a round head and are slender and tapered to a fine point. They come in several lengths. Use one which is the same measure as, or only slightly longer than, the thickness of both soles; these nails work by penetrating, striking steel and clinching, or turning back on themselves and locking in the leather. Brass clinching nails are superb. A square-faced, medium-weight hammer saves your fingers while nailing. Some sandalmakers nail from the top sole to the bottom sole and some from bottom to top. This, like arches and heels, is a personal decision. From bottom to top is often considered to be the strongest, since the nail head affords better protection against wear; but these may scratch when they get worn down a bit. Nailing from top to bottom gives a nice motif of nail heads, and I can attest to the strength of this method after having worn one pair of "top to bottom" sandals for 3 years.

The second system of attachment is to *sew* the soles together with waxed linen thread. Your shoeman can do this in 5 minutes for about $1.50 on his soling machine, or you can painstakingly do it yourself. Using the stitching groover or a sharp knife, cut a groove on the grain sides of both upper and lower soles all the way around at least ¼ inch from the edge. Use the spacing wheel to mark holes—four or five per inch—in the groove. Open holes with a harness or scratch awl and sew a lockstitch, the strongest stitch for this purpose (see Figure 3-7).

To finish the sandals, adjust the straps to the foot snugly but not too tightly. Then nail down all the ends which extend from between the soles and cut them off. With a sharp knife, trim the soles to be as nearly the same as possible and sand the edges smooth with a power sander. Those edges should be so smooth and even that the line separating the two soles should be almost invisible. Use dye or edging ink to color the edges dark brown or black and apply wax and saddle soap until they shine.

Most sandals will need a buckle or other adjustable finding, particularly those with a heel strap. An excellent sandal finding is one which is light, smooth and easy to use. Avoid large or fancy buckles; save them for handbags or, even better, for belts. To attach the buckles, use rivets or sew them on. Punch holes with a bag punch for the tongues and sew or rivet, as desired. All sandal findings should be put on the outside of the foot. They show better there and won't get caught on one another as they might if they were on the inside. Punch holes for the tongue in the other end of the strap. Make five of them, but make them only about ¼ inch apart, since the amount of adjustment is always going to be minimal. Don't leave the hole end too long. It should end only an inch or two from the last hole. One last point regarding the hole end of the strap: I've always felt it was better in terms of both design and function to have the strap pointing toward the heel. In that position, it looks less awkward; it can't get caught on things or be tripped over; and it is easier to fasten. (See Figure 5-

3 for a pictorial representation of the above explanation of sandalmaking.)

Garments

Leather clothing had a special appeal in nearly all cultures throughout history. The pursuit of this specialized craft produces beautiful examples of craftsmanship and provides a living for many workers around the world.

As previously noted, leather is processed or tanned in any of several ways to be thick or thin, hard or soft. Each leather finds its way into thousands of articles, from shoe soles to gloves. Leather that is to be used for garments is specially tanned for that purpose. You would be well advised to stick to leathers which are termed "garment" leathers, suedes or splits (see Glossary). They are thin (2 to 3-ounce) leathers, soft, resistant to stretch and can have any of several different types of finishes. The grain side is the outside of the animal and usually shows the grain, or pattern, of hair follicles; although a sueded, or nap, finish may be introduced. The flesh side is usually sueded, by abrading. A split (see Glossary) also is usually given a sueded finish. (Note that "suede" is a type of finish, not a type of leather.) Some garment leather is tanned leaving the hair of the animal intact. These are called "hair skins" and may be used in many ways (see Figure 5-4). The grain or flesh sides may be used either in or out, depending on the effect desired. If the flesh is used inside, a lining may be required.

Some very adaptable garment leathers are: buckskin, cabretta, calfskin, capeskin, chamois, deerskin, doeskin, goatskin, mocha, kidskin and pigskin.

Leather has been used for garments over the centuries for several good reasons. Many ancient cultures used every part of the animals they hunted. Food, clothing and shelter, as well as other articles like bone beads and ceremonial accoutrements, were all ren-

Figure 5-4 A "Renaissance coat" of mouton lambskin; heavy, warm and very well made. Note the piecing on the front. By Mary Powell. (Photograph by Stephan Kosiki)

dered from animals. I have previously dealt in depth with the beauty of leather. Each quality which makes leather so beautiful is found in garment leathers: the grain, the feel, the smell, the draping and molding qualities. It is also a warm, flexible, non-woven material which is quite suited for warm coats, pants and shirts. The northern cultures use leather, with fur attached, as insulation from sub-zero temperatures. In lighter weights, used for vests, skirts and shirts, it is comparable in weight and warmth to a medium-weight wool fabric.

Another reason for the frequent use of leather is its durability. Many people think of leather, especially garment leather, as being fragile, delicate, easily soiled and not worth the trouble and expense to keep it looking nice. But just as aluminum takes the form of both aluminum foil and engine blocks, leather is made in varying degrees of delicacy. Some suede jackets are ruined if rained on once; but heavy leather hunting pants will last for generations. Clothing made of almost any garment leather, if properly constructed and cared for, will serve you for many years.

Buying garment leather is unlike buying anything else, even other leathers. You need *x* amount of a material of consistent color, thickness and quality. Fabric comes by the yard in several widths, but as yet they haven't produced an animal which yields skin precisely by the square foot. The skins are usually small (9 to 10-square feet), necessitating piecing, and are irregularly shaped. The shape, size and texture (although not the color, thickness or softness) are determined by the body of the animal. Despite technological effort to produce a "material," leather is still skin, from individual animals, which tends to vary slightly in size, shape and quality. Even the mechanically controlled color and thickness is not always constant. Holes, cuts, abrasions and other imperfections are generally in evidence. While these discrepancies are disastrous for

commercial clothing companies, they should not cause the handcrafter any trouble; for the individuality of the skins enhances the handmade quality.

As previously discussed, the best way to buy leather, especially garment leather, is in

Figure 5-5 A leather ensemble. The suede skirt has been tie-dyed. Note the colored appliqué on the finished leather top (2 to 3-ounce cowhide). By Paul Goyette. (Photograph by the artist)

100

The addition of a decorative band of scrap leather turns a dime store mug into something special. By Robin Lorenz.

A hand laced, hand painted cushion. The soft organic suedes nicely offset the hard edges, probably Islamic inspired painted designs (40″ square). By Hank De Ricco. (Photograph by Rae Ann Rubenstein)

A vest and bolero pants set of sueded cowhide. The piecing in the vest makes a pleasing and refined design. By Pat Chobot. (Courtesy of Jim Martin)

person. Bring your pattern with you and fit it to the right skin. Be wary and aware of skins with cuts, holes and weak spots; but buy them if you can manage your pattern so as to avoid them. Buying in person allows you to closely match or contrast color, thickness and texture. Sort out and select skins which are only slightly larger than your pattern piece, or arrange several pieces on a larger skin, to avoid waste. Sometimes sides (averaging 22-square feet) are made into garment leather. Many pieces can be arranged on a side, yielding much less waste per piece; this is your best buy.

If it is not possible to buy in person, you have a second alternative. Mail your pattern, keeping an extra in case yours is not returned, with a note to a salesman at the leather retailer explaining exactly what you want. Explain that you would like to minimize cost by avoiding waste and ask him to select matching skins, buying imperfect ones if your pattern allows you to avoid the major irregularities. Most times the salesman does a very good job of selecting your skins, but occasionally you'll get the impression that someone is playing a very dirty trick on you. Your next letter which questions his choice will probably get a condescending reply telling you about "natural products" and how they "can't be expected to" do this or that. It's really better to select skins yourself and avoid all this. (See Chapter 2.)

Another alternative is to order more of "skin *x*" than you'll need for your purpose. If you need three skins for a vest, order five and select the best for your article. Use the two extra for other articles or piece these skins together to get a large piece of leather, which can be used in several ways.

However you buy your skins, you'll need some idea of how much to purchase. While leather comes in square feet, commercial patterns come in square yards and are square in measurement, not in configuration. To roughly estimate how much leather you'll need to correspond to a pattern, re-member that: one yard of 36-inch fabric = 9-square feet, one yard of 45-inch fabric = 11-square feet, one yard of 54-inch fabric = 13-square feet. Leather's measure is marked in square feet on the flesh side. This estimate takes into account neither the leather's uneven shape nor the holes and cuts which you must avoid. Add 20 percent for waste and your estimate will be more accurate.

As mentioned, the pattern should be fully developed before the leather is purchased. The same patternmaking techniques found in Chapter 3 apply here, but since garments are specifically fit to a specific body, an extra measure of care and fitting of the pattern is in order. Seams, darts and other ways of fitting clothing are worked in leather much the same way as they are in fabric.

You may buy patterns specifically for leather for many articles of clothing from nearly every major pattern company. Follow the same rules for buying a pattern as you would if it were to be made in cloth.

Another way of developing a pattern is to take apart an old article of clothing, iron the pieces of cloth and use them as your pattern, or transfer them to paper. Choose an article which fits and is made well. If you can't take it apart, it is possible to make a pattern with tissue paper from an assembled article. Be sure to allow ⅝ inch extra for seams and add a bit to the length of the sleeves and legs, since leather tends to develop creases and draws up more than cloth does.

Both of the above are fine ways of adapting patterns, but both rely on someone else's designs and ideas. Design variation is arrived at by changing some of the elements of a given pattern. By changing pockets, moving seams, shortening or lengthening, substituting buttons for a zipper, you are varying existing patterns and making your things unique. Using an existing pattern as a basis, you can still impose many of your own individual ideas. Eventually you may wish to design and produce clothing which is completely your own. When you do so, you are acting as a free agent, dealing with design as you see fit, developing elements and running seams anywhere, caring only about comfort and design. But you are also casting aside the good advice of the pattern companies and the practicality of a pattern which fits and flatters. A solid knowledge of sewing, patterns *and* leather is needed before you become your own designer.

Having bought or developed a pattern, by all means make a fabric mock-up first, to be absolutely sure of fit and design. You may use inexpensive muslin, an old sheet or felt, which drapes much the same as leather. You might even use rayon or other lining material for a full-sized trial. Later, you can take it in slightly and use it as the lining, since leather can cling or crock (balling up of the

Figure 5-6 An outstanding machine-sewn vest. The tailored details—bound buttonholes and pockets, seams and darts for better fit—show a thorough knowledge of leather and tailoring. Two to three-ounce waxed-finish cowhide garment leather. By Ray Memmel. (Photograph by Jeff Brooks)

Figure 5-8 Leather pants combining sueded and finished garment leathers. The seam in the knees will reduce bagging. The design of that seam is repeated in the waistband. By Robin Lorenz.

104

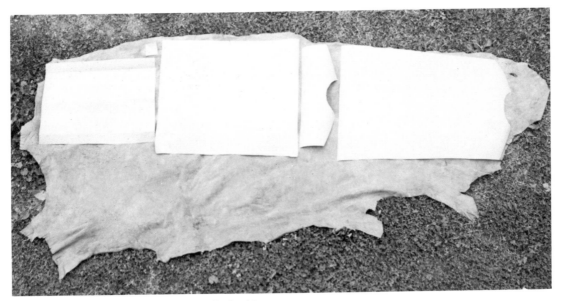

Figure 5-7 Lay pattern pieces parallel to the backbone to avoid uneven stretching of the leather.

sueded side). A lining should fit well and be free-hanging when possible. It can be tacked with thread or basting tape.

Carefully go over the leather you've bought. On the side which will face inside (as mentioned, flesh *or* grain side of garment leather may be exposed) mark all cuts, holes and weak spots with chalk. Lay out the pattern to avoid these spots when possible. Thin spots can be reinforced with iron-on tape or with glued-on leather patches. Cuts and holes can sometimes be effectively patched by skiving the edges very thin and cementing a patch of the same leather from behind. Or the patch may be emphasized with blatant stitching. This emphasis of what would normally be a defect is in keeping with leather's casual nature.

Patterns for cloth are often marked "place on fold." The cloth is then folded and cut, resulting in two mirror-imaged pieces joined at the fold, as in a shirt back. *This cannot be done in leather.* Leather cannot be doubled and then cut. You must either have a full pattern which includes both identical halves, or trace completely around the half pattern

and carefully flip that, butting up the fold lines. You may find marking with an awl is impractical. If this is so, use a ballpoint or felt tip pen.

Most heavy leathers may be cut without regard to grain or direction of pattern, allowing maximum use of the leather. Garment leather, however, being thin and soft and still subject to hard wear, must be laid out with the grain. Garment leather stretches more against the grain than with it. In a given piece of leather, there is less stretch head to tail than side to side. Pieces should be laid on the grain, parallel to the backbone of the animal. This promotes good fit and draping and minimizes wrinkling and bagging.

The leather varies within a skin. It is thickest and strongest at the neck and can be spongy and stretchy at the edges. Avoid edges in high-stress areas and put pieces which are subject to strain at the neck.

Because pattern pieces must be carefully laid in only certain places, you aren't able to arrange your pieces closely, which results in a good deal of waste. One way to minimize waste and to make the most of your leather

105

is through piecing. A large pattern piece may be gotten onto two small skins by cutting that pattern in half and adding ⅝ inch to each half for overlap. Besides piecing for practical reasons, you may also wish to piece for aesthetic reasons, to individualize your work. You needn't piece only on mid-lines, or even in straight lines. A ragged-edged, too-short piece may be added, leaving the edge and the nature of the material quite evident. Piecing causes and depends on seams. These seams can be used to fit an article closely or to reduce bagging in areas of high stress, such as the knee and elbow. Seams at these points will strengthen these areas, minimizing the bagging which is unavoidable in most clothing, whether it be of cloth, leather or other material. Later, if bagging knees become too objectionable, they can be taken in at that seam with a minimum of trouble.

Mark the leather, as always, on the reverse side. Cut carefully with a mat knife or large shears, being sure the leather does not slip or fold. If you are using a hair skin, cut through the skin only, from the flesh side, with a razor.

A variety of construction techniques is open to you. Garments may be hand or machine sewn, or hand laced or thonged. Although any system can be used, I prefer the hand thonging. Currently in vogue are thonged chamois garments, to be seen in many New York City shops. They are lovely, unique and elaborate and have a much stronger handmade appeal than their machine sewn counterparts. While the technique is similar to handsewing, the effect is much more pleasing. Quarter-inch thongs of the same leather are made from circles cut in spirals, or from a straight edge. A large-eye needle or any lacing needle draws the thong through pre-punched holes, creating any of the previously mentioned thonging patterns.

Heavy duty cotton, cotton-wrapped polyester or linen threads are used in handsewing. Holes may be punched and a needle may be used to make the seams and stitches, as in Figure 5-10. More often, a glover's needle is used to sew garments. No hole is punched, for this three-sided needle cuts its own. Eight to ten stitches to the inch is usual, but Furry Foote, a Minnesota Cree (see Figures 5-14 and 5-15), averages forty to the inch.

Machine sewing, while certainly much faster than any hand method, is correspondingly less handmade looking. A thorough knowledge of sewing and sewing machines is mandatory, as is an instruction booklet for your particular machine.

Both electric and treadle machines will sew leather, the latter being perhaps the more versatile. Many leatherworkers feel that electric machines give speed and require less physical labor to operate, but are not as easily controlled. The foot-operated machines, although they take more energy to use, are more easily managed. They are also built very simply, designed to handle everything from muslin to heavy canvas, and are easily adjustable. The artisan becomes completely one with the treadle machine, as the aesthetic and the technical combine. This aspect of handcraft is unique and thoroughly enjoyable.

Use a walking or rolling presser foot and a size 16 to 19 needle with cotton, silk or linen thread set at seven to nine stitches to the inch. Before sewing, baste the leather together with rubber cement, paper clips or tape (not pins, which leave holes), to keep it from slipping or stretching. Fit it to the figure once more and make final adjustments. Both threads should be under the presser foot and the leading edge of the leather should come under the needle just far enough to catch the first stitch. Stop just before going off the edge, remove the piece, and tie and tuck in the ends. Later, you can add a few hand stitches or a rivet for reinforcement. Don't backstitch, as it cuts the leather. To protect finished leather from the teeth of the feed dog, sew on paper which you can tear off later.

Hems are not often taken, because leather does not ravel, and the raw edge enhances the natural look of the material. Darts should

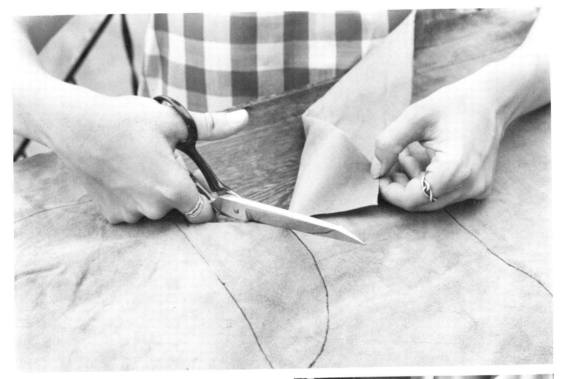

Figure 5-9 Having marked garment leather, you may cut it with shears.

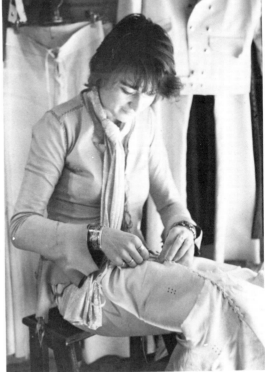

be flattened, sewn, trimmed and the edges cemented to the body of the piece. Seams are treated in the same manner.

Remember when machine sewing to go slowly and carefully. This type of sewing goes much faster than any handsewing, but don't neglect to be as careful here as you would be with any aspect of leatherwork, for carelessness will show in the end.

Leather garments need care, just as all other clothing does. It is not, however, the finicky material which many think it is. Don't let a leather garment get filthy before it is

Figure 5-10 A leather artisan, Anouchka B. Mayer, thonging leather garments in her New York shop.

107

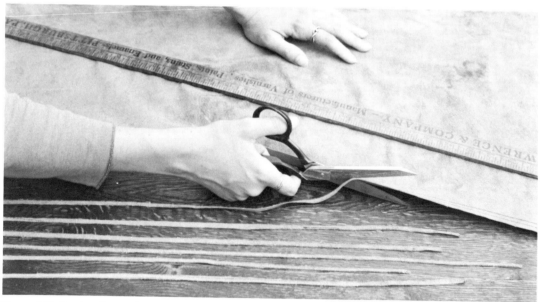

Figure 5-11 Cutting thongs from a straight edge with shears.

Figure 5-12 Carefully punching holes to receive thongs. Note the guideline which keeps holes the same distance from the edge.

108

Figure 5-13 A leather tunic of 2 to 3-ounce chrome-tanned cowhide, with pewter buttons. The X-stitch, sewn twice, resulted in the strong woven seams. By Nancy Edwards.

Figure 5-14 Deer and sheepskin, beads and buttons are used in these leather garments and moccasins. They have rustic spontaneity and strong design; a rare combination. By Furry Foote. (Photograph by the artist)

Figure 5-16 A black pigskin swimming suit. Water has little or no effect on some leathers. Note the front closure which is very much like that on a tie shoe. By Jeff Brooks.

cleaned. As a rule, have leather garments professionally cleaned annually. Water will not damage most garment leathers unless they are completely saturated. Hang to dry in a cool area and brush suede in one direction with a sponge when dry. If the leather has become dried and brittle due to the wetting, revitalize with a commercial conditioner. Avoid wrinkling garments by hanging them separately. Remove wrinkles by hanging or by pressing with an iron set at its lowest heat, using heavy paper as insulation.

Figure 5-15 A deerskin shirt combining grain and flesh sides of the leather, fabric and beads in a spontaneous design. This artist uses no patterns and sews forty stitches to the inch. By Furry Foote. (Photograph by the artist)

Chapter 6
Miscellaneous Projects

Furniture

From the thrones of ancient kings to the outstanding contemporary work of Federico Armijo, leather has been used in furniture, once again, because of the unique qualities it offers the craftsman. It is strong, durable, flexible, moldable and available in many weights for many purposes. It pleases all senses, especially when used in large expanses such as in furniture. The feel of leather is unique, for it is often both hard and soft at the same time. It goes "crunch" when you sit in a leather chair. It shines with a deep luster and shows off the beautiful grain and coloring. Even the smell of leather is unique and characteristic.

Leather has excellent working properties which are well suited for furniture. Nearly any weight leather can be formed into any shape and the construction techniques (thonging, sewing) add to its earthy appeal. A piece of furniture is planned so that all pieces work together in the design. Note the strong design qualities in the furniture pictured in this chapter. A sculptural form is built of cut and polished wood and leather, one serving to verify and complement the other. Note too how carefully the texture, finish and color of these pieces are integrated; the warm, shining, grained wood surfaces form a nice counterpoint to the equally refined leather pieces.

Leather may be used as upholstery: either for covering a soft stuffing (see Figure 6-2) or as a single, free-hanging thickness (see Figure 6-3). The frame of a piece may be the major element, with leather as an accent. A piece may also be comprised totally of leather with no frame at all, as in a "bean-bag" chair, or the leather may totally enclose the frame, as in Figure 6-4. Leather may also be inlayed, or patched and affixed, to a wooden backing which may be the top of a table (see Figure 6-5).

Chairs, stuffed chairs, ottomans, couches, pillows, tables, stools and other pieces may be completely or partly made of leather. Some articles do not require a frame, but most need some sort of armature. Wood and metal are the most common materials for frames, with the former being used more often.

Figure 6-1 Matched chairs: the one on the left is a rocker. The saddle skirting the leather is joined to the oak frames with slots, loops and pegs. By Federico Armijo. (Photograph by the artist)

Figure 6-2 A contemporary rocking chair: stuffed 2 to 3-ounce garment leather pouches form the seat and back. The knob at the bottom is a counterbalance for the rocking inner frame. By Hunter Kariher. (Courtesy of the artist)

Metal frames may be made of aluminum (as the hanging chair in Figure 6-4), brass, steel or other metals. Enclosed or exposed metal frames are bolted and wired together, or are heliarced, brazed or welded, respectively. The finish on these metals can be left as is, covered with leather or given a clear or colored lacquer finish. Brass and steel can even be chrome plated. The advantages of metal frames are that a "slick" result can be obtained relatively easily and the material is abundant and easily worked. Few specialized tools are required and complex fabrication like welding can be, and often is, sent out to a metal fabricator to be performed. In addition, the frame will be very strong. Disadvantages are excessive weight, some difficulty in attaching leather to the frame and the sometimes disunified look of leather and metal.

Wood gives the handworker more leeway and a great probability of success. It, too, is easily worked, although certain tools are necessary. A variety of woods is available and suitable for frames; they are strong, relatively light in weight, durable and with an even grain which finishes beautifully. Some excellent woods which complement leather and may be cut and milled or purchased at a hardwood lumberyard are maple, oak, cherry, mahogany, teak, birch and walnut. When textures, grains and colors of these and other woods are combined with leather, good results are nearly guaranteed.

Wood joints may be relatively easily executed. Some of the more basic are the cross lap joint, mortise and tenon joint, dowel pin joint, miter joint and dovetail joint. Specifics may be found in a woodworking text. For a permanent bond, use plastic resin glue. For an excellent bond which can be taken apart, use hide glue.

All woods, like leather, should be given a finish to protect and enhance the beauty of the natural wood. One is applied only after the wood is sanded smooth (with the grain) with several courses of sandpaper, until all saw marks and scratches are removed. Common

finishes include linseed oil, shellac, varnish and stain, applied in various combinations. A newly developed polyurethane sealer which is virtually indestructible is available. It shows off the wood like shellac, yet completely protects it and never needs touchups. The finish I prefer to use is an oil stain, which is a colored stain carried in oil. Applied generously in two or more coats, the oil finishes and protects the wood while the stain emphasizes the grain. Oil stains are available in many colors to match many woods, although you can finish a wood with a stain other than one designed for it.

Figure 6-3 One piece of heavy leather supports the sitter in this high-backed black walnut chair. By Federico Armijo. (Photograph by the artist)

113

Figure 6-4 A swing of various leathers and furs envelops an aluminum frame. Large enough for two, it hangs and swings on chains. By Libby Platus. (Photograph by Phil Shuper)

114

Figure 6-5 An oak and leather table consisting of many shapes, types and colors of 4 to 8-ounce leather, inlayed and affixed to a wooden backing. By the author.

Followed by several coats of paste wax and buffed to a sheen, the wood will be beautifully finished and relatively well protected.

This chapter cannot present more than a very basic introduction to the intricate craft of woodworking. Your choice of woods, working procedures and finishes depends on various woods' qualities and your needs, perhaps even more so than your choice of leathers. An excellent text on woodworking which should help you immensely and answer every question is *The Complete Woodworking Handbook* by Jeanette T. Adams and Emanuele Stieri (Arco Publishing Co.).

The leather you choose will depend on your design. If your intended use is for upholstery, the leather should be thin, strong and flexible. Most garment leathers or suede splits one to three-ounce will work quite nicely. A pouch or pillow is formed and stuffed with foam rubber, or the traditional method of upholstering with springs and webbing is followed. If your design calls for leather which forms the seat and/or back or which must, in some other way, support weight without itself being supported, the leather should be heavy with a minimum of stretch. Six to eight-ounce vegetable-tanned cowhide is the best for this purpose. Most harness and saddle leather is excellent.

Several systems are used to attach leather to the frame. With a wood or metal frame, the leather may simply be sewn around a crosspiece. Grommets may be evenly spaced around the edge and the leather can be laced to the frame. Or a slot may be formed in the frame which a loop of leather fits through. A peg through this loop will hold it securely. Leather may be attached to wood in additional ways. It can be tacked with brass up-

115

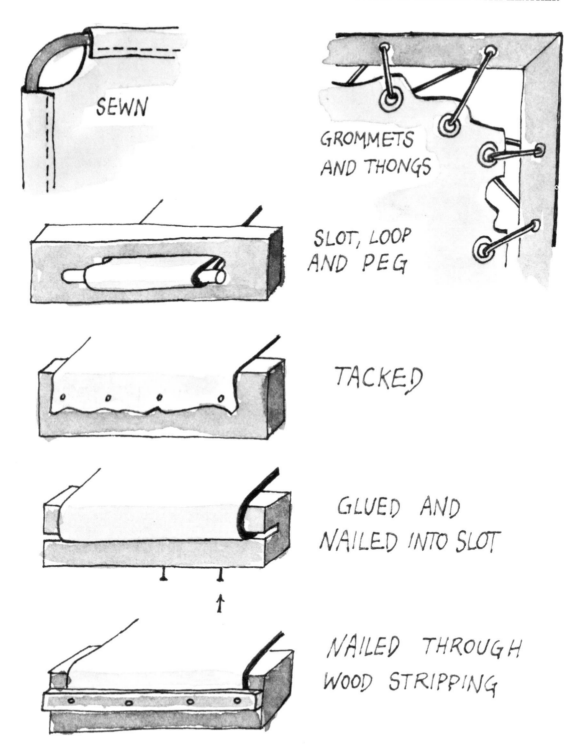

SEWN

GROMMETS
AND THONGS

SLOT, LOOP
AND PEG

TACKED

GLUED AND
NAILED INTO SLOT

NAILED THROUGH
WOOD STRIPPING

Figure 6-6 Many systems attractively and effectively
hold leather to a frame.

holstery nails, glued and nailed into a slot, or can be held by nails which penetrate both leather and an outside stripping which hides raw edges (see Figure 6-6).

The design and construction of leather furniture are dependent upon one another. The design is decided upon within the restrictions of the pieces and the way they are put together. As with all leather goods, both design and construction are further restricted by function, which varies with the numerous types of furniture. These "restrictions" are not restraints to be rebelled against, but are conditions necessary to development of imagination.

Taking the example of a wood and leather chair, the function, design and construction might be developed thus:

Function: A comfortable rocking chair, framed with wood, with unsupported leather as seat and back.

Design: Only square stock is to be used and all angles in wood and leather will be 90° except where comfort necessitates.

Construction: Mortise and tenon joints will be used, being best suited to the function and design. Leather will be 6-ounce vegetable-tanned cowhide, joined to the maple frame with slots, loops and pegs. Rocking action will be achieved with a double frame, the outer one supporting, with a fulcrum, the inner one which holds the leather.

These considerations must be further correlated and integrated and sketching should begin. Once a working design has been achieved, a scale model will be built to assure proper proportion and design. The final product should begin only after extensive thought, research and planning.

Leather Art

Used in articles from belts to chamois shirts, each leather finds one or more applications. This text, so far, has discussed the practical or functional side of leatherworking: the making of usable objects from various skins.

There is a whole other realm of expression, though, into which I will delve only summarily. That "other side" of leather handcraft is the production of art objects.

The articles dealt with thus far are alike in that I have encouraged functionality, but with a flair for design. The objectives and results are different with art objects. The piece must have a total oneness with the material from which it is made. The theme must be carried smoothly through the material, transcending mechanical or manual construction. The idea or theme must blend with and envelop the production and the material which is used. In a way, many artists are super-craftsmen. They have gone so far beyond ordinary technical problems that they are able to use a given medium as a material of expression. My purposes in this chapter are not to accept or reject art forms or styles, but to open the door to new methods of expression. Your art will be your own, if your ideas and intentions are unique.

Leather has several qualities which made it very suitable for artistic undertakings. There are many kinds, of varying colors, sizes, shapes and thicknesses. All leather is flexible (in varying degrees), resilient and extremely durable. The appearance of any given leather, and sometimes its physical properties, can be changed or modified by the application of dye, oil, heat or water. Some leathers will drape like fabric and some are as hard as wood. Leather can be used flat or one-dimensionally or can be molded into three-dimensional forms. The earthy, sensuous appeal of leather is not to be discounted. The combination of these qualities makes it a variable material indeed.

Combine the above qualities with leather's ability to blend with and complement many materials and a host of design possibilities will present themselves. As we've seen, leather goes quite well with rough or polished wood, brass, copper, bone, ceramic, fibers, cork and other materials which have their own intrinsic appeal and complemen-

Figure 6-7 A twelve foot tall wall sculpture using knotted, wrapped and stretched leathers and rope. By Libby Platus (pictured). (Photograph by Jack Koehler)

Classic leatherwork, using oak tanned leather and aniline dyes. The design is created in the traditional method, with modeling and repoussé, impressing from behind. By Dick Young. (Photograph by Tom Bieber)

Matching (36″ square) ottomans. Colored suedes are inlayed, laced and painted with aniline dye and acrylic paint. By Hank De Ricco. (Photograph by Rae Ann Rubenstein)

Leather lends itself to many types of expression. "Grandma's House," a wall hanging of macraméd leather strips and string. By Libby Platus. (Photograph by Virginia Black)

tary qualities. Leather may also be used to good advantage in combination with other leathers. You can use two and three types, weights or colors in a single piece. This quality is generally not true of other media, such as wood or stone.

In the creation of leather art, you are dealing with physical appearances more than actual functions. While the piece need not perform a useful task, as would all the other items discussed in this book, it must, by the same token, be of outstanding conception, design and construction. Techniques of fabrication and embellishment, as well as materials, tools and their application, are the same as in other leatherwork. But in this application, construction and design elements must serve as an integral part of the artistic plan. While stitches or rivets still hold the piece together, the appearance now has priority. Ordinarily, I will lace only where two or more pieces need to be joined and not as

an arbitrary applied design. The design freedom in art pieces gives the license to add embellishments where desired, regardless of function or lack thereof. The construction techniques become designs which must function with, and can greatly enhance, the theme, line and handling of the piece. (See Chapter 3, on secondary design and design coordination.) Here is the place to use the tricks of the trade you will learn: the slick

Figure 6-8 The combination of textures and colors of highly polished leather, bone, horn and a convex mirror form a striking "Hog-Jaw Mirror" (12″ × 15″). By Nancy Flanagan. (Photograph by Floyd Flanagan)

Figure 6-9 A large (3′ × 1¾′) wall hanging which has been painstakingly and flawlessly tooled. It is outstanding in that the traditional tooling is in complete harmony with the contemporary forms which make up the piece. By John Coutoupis.

leather fastenings, leather buttons, fancy braiding. You will learn these, and many more tricks through careful study of modern and classic leatherwork.

"Tricks of the trade," or highly designed functional elements, must be tastefully done or the piece will appear to be a jumble of ideas. Even in the boldest, crudest art, a delicate combination, of the elements and components of art is mandatory for good results. The elements include color, space, shape, line, form, value and texture. The compo-

nents include subject matter, organization and interpretation. The "organization" is quite specific, dealing with harmony, proportion, balance, rhythm, variety, unity and emphasis. A more thorough discussion is not, unfortunately, permitted by space or intent of this book. A detailed account may be found in a good art text.

As confusing as these elements and components sound, they are actually concise definitions of vague feelings which we all have. When you buy a hat, you do so because

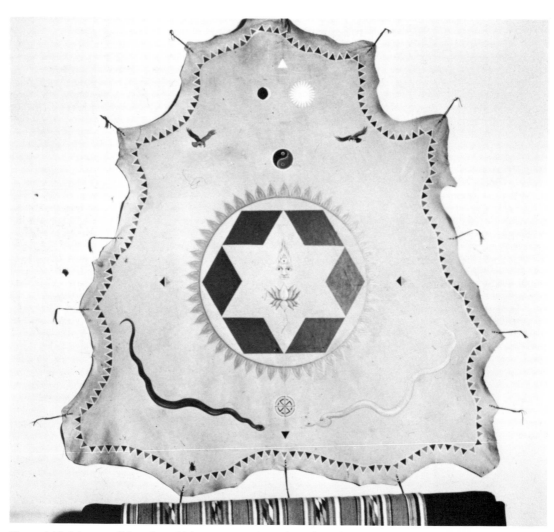

Figure 6-10 A large wall hanging which uses an entire skin. Symbols from many cultures, religions and sects have been hand painted. By Hank De Ricco. (Photograph by Rae Ann Rubenstein)

Figure 6-11 In this study for a large mural, a strong three-dimensional design has been created with stretched goatskin formed into elements of various sizes and shapes. By Caroline Montague. (Courtesy of the artist)

Figure 6-12 Two-ounce kip, tooled four-ounce vegetable-tanned cowhide and seven-ounce yellow latigo are combined with oil stained maple and a photograph in this wall hanging entitled "Flying Scarab." By the author.

123

Figure 6-13 Note the design details on this necklace made of copper and several types of leather. By the author.

something about it pleases you. A hat is not art, but you are exercising the same feelings for design, texture and line. Don't be wary of the above definitions. They define qualities which we all possess. Try to develop these qualities through experimentation. Look through your scraps and pick out pieces which please you because of texture, design, color or whatever. Decide what you wish to make. Develop an idea for the piece. It may

Figure 6-14 A delicate pattern of positive and negative shapes is created with 2 to 3-ounce sueded and finished leathers and bone, silver and turquoise beads. Note the natural edges (48″ in diameter). By Judy La Fon. (Photograph by Mark La Fon)

be an exercise on a theme or it may be a statement by itself, or simply an object which pleases your senses.

When I set out to make a leather necklace such as those shown in Figure 6-15, I know basically what I'm going to make. I have a general idea of the design, but I try not to let that idea restrict me. Searching through the scrap reservoir, I find pieces which please me and combine them in what I consider to be unique ways. By lacing, cutting, a little sewing or gluing, and through combinations of shapes, colors, lines and textures, I de-

Figure 6-16 A cool control is extended in this piece where wood and leather shapes resemble, reflect and flow from one another. By Caroline Montague. (Courtesy of the artist)

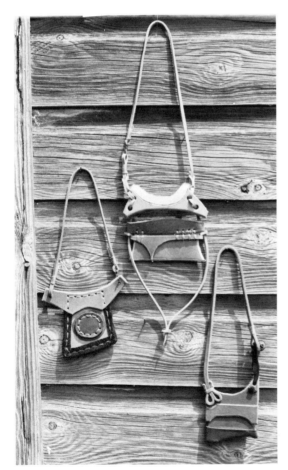

Figure 6-15 Leather necklaces made of all weights and tannages combined with other materials, such as copper, fur and linen thread in intricate designs. By the author.

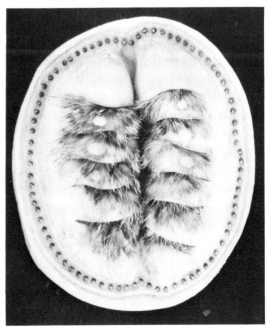

Figure 6-17 Leather is used as a medium of expression when rawhide, fur and paint are combined to make this "Rawhide Fetish" (4¼″ × 4¾″). By Nancy Flanagan. (Photograph by Floyd Flanagan)

125

velop a strong design while balancing the elements and components of art.

A painting professor once told me that art was the only thing which people bought simply to look at, to reflect on their own thoughts and those of the artist. Another, closer friend once remarked that, "Art is All." In the light of these two valid statements, perhaps we can see how an artist strives to give vent and life to his emotions and ideas, which are sometimes carefully ar-ranged, sometimes not, through his art. Stone, plaster, wood, plastic, steel, rope, clay, cloth, leather and more are all materials or media. They each have certain unique qualities and characteristics which should be used to the hilt. Remember that each of these materials is a medium of expression and has its strengths, qualities and limits. Choose your medium carefully and be sure that it has the qualities you need and that you have the ability to bring them to life.

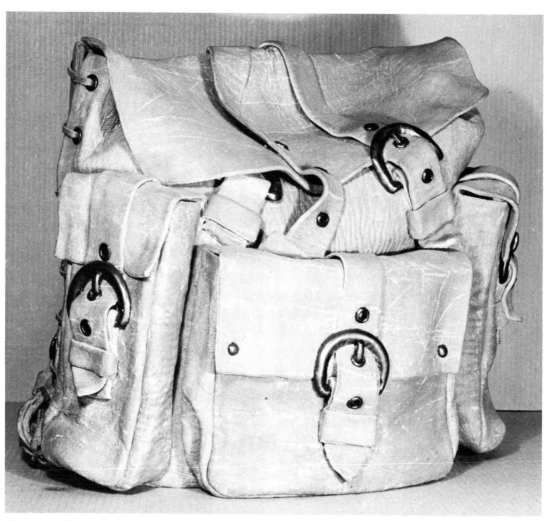

Figure 6-18 The medium here is ceramic. Leather's every distinctive feature is captured here in this "Knapsack." By Marilyn Levine. (Photograph by the artist)

Don't use a material in a way which contradicts its nature and don't fool yourself into believing that because an article is made of a beautiful material it must be art. Art depends on a delicate balance between idea and execution.

The photographs in this chapter are all individual expressions, whether of theme, idea or design. Observe colors, textures, embellishments, methods of joining pieces and the overall design in all leather goods whether in a book or in a museum. Experiment. Remember that the validity of your art depends not only on your ability to handle the medium, but on your individual design innovation.

Using Scraps Profitably

If you have made any or all the previously described articles, you will undoubtedly have a goodly supply of "spontaneous reserve raw material," otherwise known as

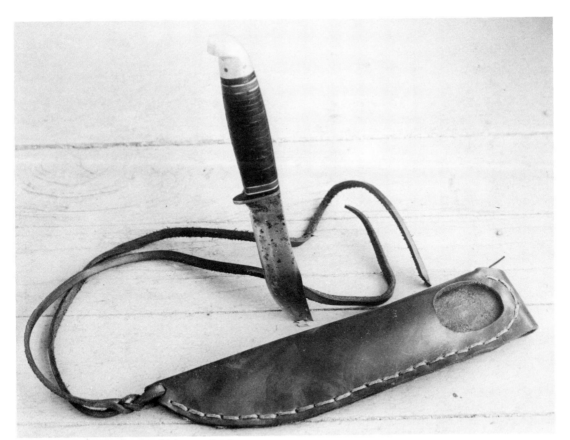

Figure 6-19 A knife sheath which completely encases the knife. It is made, complete with belt loop, of one piece of yellow latigo, 7 to 8-ounce. It was handsewn and hand dyed with waxed linen thread. By the author.

scrap. I have about two bushels of spontaneous reserve raw material waiting for me in the basement. Its judicious use can result in much more leather for your dollars. You simply cannot afford to waste raw material which costs something above $1 a square foot, and usually more like $1.50. But how to use them?

The economy-minded and aesthetic-minded artisan recognizes the need to use leather in the best possible manner. This includes not only the design and construction of a given piece, but also the careful use of materials. Arrange your pattern pieces so that you use the leather as economically as possible. Butt up straight-edged pieces. Without being stingy, fit as many pattern pieces into a given space as possible. Luckily, patterns may be laid on most leathers in any direction without regard to grain, so you may thereby utilize a maximum amount of leather. Exceptions to this are light leathers, such as garment suedes, and heavily creased or grained leathers.

In any case, lay out your pattern pieces so as to save the most leather. Try to keep the hide in one piece. If you must cut a piece (which will become scrap) away from the body of the hide, make it either quite large or quite small. Either way, you'll at least make an attempt at saving leather. Arrange your pieces on the leather several ways before you mark them for cutting. Compare arrangements and decide which saves the most leather. Nothing is more frustrating than needing one more piece of leather to complete a bag and having only a piece with a hole in the very middle, which you cut in a thoughtless moment. If you need a small piece, cut it from a piece which is only slightly larger. This will save your large scraps for larger applications.

Save all your scraps. In no time at all, you will have amassed a small warehouse of bits and pieces of leather of all weights, tannages, colors and sizes. These are valuable resource materials for leather art and these scraps can act as a catalogue of the leathers you have used in the past, aiding future selection.

Another consideration in the use of scrap is time. Everybody knows that time is money and the time you spend making watch fobs of questionable quality, only to use the scrap, may be better spent making a pair of sandals. What a paradox: you can't afford to use scraps and you can't afford not to use them!

The first trick is to avoid creating scrap. Once you make scrap, not only is your money tied up in hard-to-find-a-use-for material, but you always know it's just lying around waiting for you! To effectively use scrap, you must design articles which you can make quickly, using small pieces of leather. Leather is a material which seems to work best in large articles. When used in small quantities, the grain and texture are less apparent. It often loses its appeal and might as well be synthetic.

BARRETTES

One standard scrap project is the making of barrettes. These are small pieces of leather which are used to tie the hair back. Barrettes of this sort are attractive, useful and have been in fashion for years.

Barrettes can be cut in almost any shape. Let the already cut or raw edges of your scraps suggest unique shapes to you. Any leather, any tannage, from 4 to 8-ounce, will work well. The size should be roughly 4 by 2½ inches, but this is an approximation and slightly larger or smaller will probably work as well. As mentioned, don't stick only to ovals, rectangles and crescents. Let the shape of the scrap influence the shape of the barrette.

There are two types of leather barrettes. Both hold the hair with a wooden stick, but in slightly differently ways. One type has two holes through which the stick passes. Between the holes there remains a small space which seems just made for decoration, whether by tooling, dyeing, incising or riveting. A second type has one large hole, usually oval, which frames the hair as the major

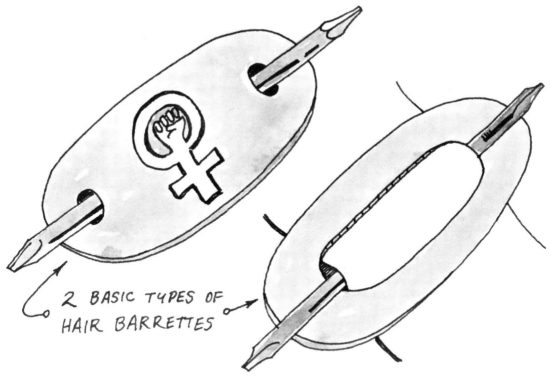

2 BASIC TYPES OF HAIR BARRETTES

Figure 6-20 Hair barrettes are an attractive and functional way to use scraps.

decoration (see Figure 6-20). The holes in the first barrette are made with a ¼-inch or larger drive punch, or with a bag punch, used once to give a slot, or twice in an "X" pattern. The hole in the second type is cut with an oval arch punch or carefully with a mat knife.

The sticks are made from ¼-inch dowel rods which you cut into 3½ to 4½-inch lengths. (I've tried whittling my own from boards, but they are quite time-consuming and the end product normally breaks.) The ends of the dowels are sharpened. Some people use a pencil sharpener, but I find this too mechanical-looking; and it also makes the barrette a dangerous weapon. I prefer to irregularly sharpen the ends with three or four cuts of a sharp knife and nick the stick slightly to give it a "rustic" quality. Leather dye or wood stain is then applied for color.

To avoid coloring your fingers, hold the sticks and dye only one-half the length. Let this dry and repeat the operation on the other end. You may use a dauber or dip the sticks directly in the bottle.

Make your barrettes different sizes, with the holes spaced differently too, and make the sticks of different lengths, since people who wear barrettes have different amounts and weights of hair and these barrettes aren't adjustable.

BRACELETS, WRISTBANDS AND OTHER ITEMS
Bracelets, wristbands, watchbands, necklaces and chokers are also good ways to use scrap profitably. All of these are small items and must be delicately or at least carefully made. (A loose watchband will not be worn.)

129

They must also be nonabrasive, as leather can be. From a design standpoint, these articles need to be well proportioned and tastefully made. On a small article such as a choker, small details or embellishments are in order. Fit your decorations to the piece, but don't overuse them. The thonging which looks fine on a handbag is out of place on a watchband. The trick braid, tooling, dyeing or a pattern of rivets can be effective decoration for any of these bands, which can be made from practically any leather from 2 to 8-ounce. Don't overlook the use of colored suedes.

To make any of these bands fasten, you will need snaps, buckles, thongs or leather buttons. The buttons look very nice but are not handy to use. They work very well in fabric, but leather tends to bind over a leather button. The buckle is the most positive lock and should be used on the watchband; but the snap looks very nice and is the easiest to apply and use.

Of all these bands, the watchband is the most difficult to make. In fact, it may be one of the trickiest things for a leatherworker. Its physical requirements call for a unique combination of leathers and hardware: it must fit smoothly and snugly without binding, must lock with a buckle and be easy to fasten and unfasten. The watch itself must be securely fastened to the band but must be removable. The leather you use must be quite strong and thin. One good way to make a strong, simple watchband is to use a 2 to 3-ounce strap of cow, horse, calf or goatskin of the proper width to hold the buckle, watch and holes and to use a thicker (5 to 8-ounce) piece to hold this strap (see Figure 6-21).

There are other bands besides the above which may be made from scrap. Hatbands whether made from snakeskin or cowhide are nice. Put leather shapes together on a leather string, or make them out of one continuous piece. Cut a hole in each end of a

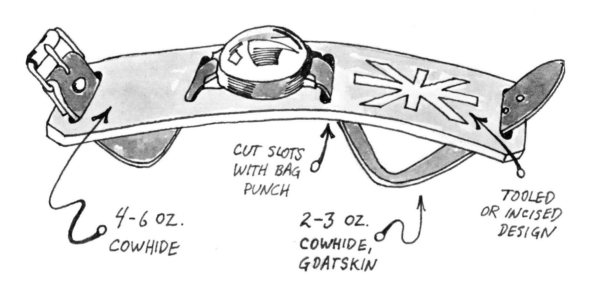

Figure 6-21 Construction of a simple leather watchband.

130

Figure 6-22 Hand dyed yellow latigo (2¼" squares) sewn with waxed linen, with an oak border to form the chessboard for the unglazed ceramic chessmen. By the author.

hatband and run a leather string through to make it adjustable.

A decorated and polished leather band which snaps around a dime store beer mug makes it a "good" mug (see color insert).

If you have made a lot of belts or handbags, you may have many strap scraps—pieces which are 1 to 2 inches wide and 6 or more inches long. These can be joined together to make a full-size belt either by skiving the ends and joining leather to leather or by joining each piece with a ring between. It is best to make the most of each situation. Since you have a belt made of many pieces, emphasize the construction. Dye each a different color or decorate each piece differently.

In the same vein, if you have been making garments and have a lot of different colored garment leather scraps, try cutting geometric shapes and joining them, like a patchwork quilt. You will have a large, multicolor piece of leather from which to make a bag or even a garment. Be sure, however, that the leathers you piece together are of approximately the same weight. If one is substantially heavier or lighter than the others, or if many weights of leather are used, uneven stresses will be developed causing unnatural puckering, gapping and creasing.

Piecing has many applications. The leather chessboard with ceramic men in Figure 6-22 could have been inlaid into a table top. The leather in the table in Figure 6-5 was made from scraps of various leathers.

Another type of patch is one for clothing. Small lightweight leather patches will outlive

131

the fabrics they are patching and will survive numerous washings. These clothing patches may be used functionally: to mend a tear at the knee; to rework straight pant legs into bells by adding a leather insert; or decoratively, as in a design of appliquéd colored suedes.

There are many other uses for scrap, from shoelaces to medallions to something for the dog to chew. Save all but your smallest scraps for future use when the need arises. Plan to use them in leather jewelry and art, or use pieces of different weight, texture or color leathers to give life to what might otherwise be a dull purse. A leather closure is imaginative and a good combination with a leather bag. A plain purse could have a bright suede design appliquéd on the flap. By combining leathers of slightly different hues or textures in a single bag, you add another design dimension. If you just can't find any other use for scrap, you can cut it into leather thongs and spirals to put together a suitcase or two.

I always keep spontaneous reserve raw material for several reasons. It is sound business from an economic standpoint; and saving scrap allows you to have many different types of leather to use, even if they are sometimes in rather small pieces. But the most important reason why I keep all my scrap material is that while looking for a particular leather, I always come upon unused, accidentally cut, left over but beautifully shaped odd bits which help to inspire my imagination and spur my creativity.

Figure 6-23 A wet-formed leather box is completely covered with small pieces of colored suedes and fur. By Ron Kwiatkowski. (Photograph by James Utter)

Appendix

Glossary of Leather Terms

Alligator A general term for leather made of all aquatic species with a grain similar to the American alligator, which cannot be killed legally and is not used in the United States.

Alligator Grained Leather A term distinguishing the alligator grain effect embossed on various cattle or sheep leathers from the genuine reptilian leather.

Alum Leather Leather produced by alum tannage, in combination with salt, egg yolk and other materials. Now used chiefly for glove leather, this was once the most prevalent tanning method.

Aniline-Dyed Leather Leather dyed with aniline dyes, as opposed to those colored with pigments and other opaque materials.

Antelope Finish Suede Lambskin, goatskin or calfskin, sueded and finished to resemble antelope.

Antelope Leather A rare, soft, velvety fine leather made from antelope skin.

Back Formed by cutting the hide longitudinally along the backbone, then trimming off head and belly, leaving a "bend" and shoulder.

Bark Tannage Describes leather preserved with tannins in barks, wood and other plant derivatives as distinguished from mineral tannages.

Basil Uncolored vegetable-tanned sheep and lambskins.

Bating A chemical process to remove the lime from the skin and to prepare it for actual tanning.

Belly A stretchy, inferior leather from the underside of the animal.

Belt Leathers A good quality leather for waist belts.

Belting Leather Butts of high grade cattlehide used for leather belts to transmit power in machinery.

Bend A sole leather "back" minus the shoulder.

Blue Applied to skins or hides that have been chrome-tanned but not finished.

Boarding Graining by folding the leather and rubbing grain to grain, producing soft, creased leather.

Bookbinding Leather Leather to bind books: skivers, splits, cowhides, sheepskins, goatskins, calf and sealskins.

Bridle Leather Strong, soft, curried vegetable-tanned cowhide.

Buckskin A general term for leather from deer and elk skins. The un-split skin, minus the surface grain, is "genuine buckskin"; a split is "split buckskin."

Buck Sides Cattlehide upper shoe leather, with a grain buffed to simulate buckskin.

Buff Hides Country hides weighing 45 to 60 pounds untrimmed, 43 to 58 pounds trimmed.

Buffalo Leather Leather tanned from the domesticated water buffalo of the Far East (not the American bison).

Buffing Abrasion with an emery wheel to produce a fine nap or minimize irregularities.

Butt Part of the hide covering the animal's hindquarters.

Cabretta Sheepskins having hair rather than wool coats.

Calfskin A fine distinct-grained leather made from the skins of young cattle.

Capeskin Leather with the natural grain preserved made from sheepskin, used for gloves and garments.

133

Carpincho Classed as a pigskin, this is actually leather from the hide of a South American water rodent.

Casing The dampening and mellowing of vegetable-tanned leather by slow drying.

Cattlehide Leathers Leathers from the skins of cows, steers and bulls, sometimes kips.

Chamois A very soft, oil-tanned, suede-finished leather, originally from Alpine antelope, but now made from sheepskin splits.

Chestnut Extract An agent used to tan heavy harness and sole leathers, obtained from the wood of the chestnut tree.

Chrome Tannage A rapid tanning method which is currently the most popular, using chromium salts as the tanning agent.

Colorado Steers Side-branded steer hides not necessarily from Colorado.

Combination Tannage The tanning of leather in one agent, then the re-tanning in another, to impart favorable qualities of both systems.

Cordovan Leather Originally leather from Cordoba, Spain, this term now refers to a strong, nonporous shoe leather made from a kidney-shaped section of horse butts.

Country Hides Hides, normally of inferior quality, which are removed by butchers and farmers.

Cowhide Leather A term which loosely refers to leather from any animal of the bovine species.

Crocking The balling up or rubbing off of coloring, finishing materials or residual buffing dust from leather (especially suede) onto other materials.

Crocodile Skin from this reptile is so tough that only the belly is tanned.

Crop A "side" minus only the belly, retaining head and shoulder.

Crushed Leather A leather whose natural grain has been accentuated by mechanical means.

Currying A process of incorporating oils and greases into a leather to make it suitable for a specific use.

Deacon The quite small skin of a newborn calf.

Deep Buff The first cut under the top grain, when leather is split. No traces of grain remain.

Deerskin A leather with the grain surface intact, not removed like buckskins.

Degrained Leathers Leather sueded on the flesh side. The grain is removed by splitting after tanning.

Doeskin The soft, supple formaldehyde and alum-tanned skivers of sheep and lambs. Skin of a doe is rarely used.

Dyeing The coloring of leather by flowing, spraying, dipping or immersing.

Electrified Lambskin Dyed and processed sheepskin shearlings finished to resemble fur skins.

Elk A trade term for cattlehide shoe leather of special tannage and finish. Genuine elk leather is made into one of several types of buckskins.

Embossed Leathers Leathers upon which a design (usually the natural grain of other animal skins) has been stamped with engraved plates.

Fancy Leathers All kinds of leathers which have a value and commercial importance because of grain or distinctive finish, whether natural or processed.

Fat Liquor A mixture of oils and soaps which make a leather flexible by lubricating the fibers.

Flesher A flesh-side layer split from a sheepskin before tanning.

Fleshing Removal of tissue and fat from flesh side of raw hide.

Formaldehyde Tanning A tanning process which yields white, washable, lightweight leathers using formaldehyde as the agent.

French Kid Kidskin tanned by the alum or vegetable process. Originated in France.

French Antelope Lambskin Suede leathers made from South American and New Zealand pickled lambskins.

Frigorifico Hides Brine cured and salted hides shipped for tanning to the United States by South American freezing plants.

Frog Small, thin, very fine skins of frogs. They are rarely tanned or used.

Full Grain Leather First cut taken from the hair side of a hide from which only the hair and epidermis have been removed.

Garment Leather Leather from any of several animals which has been tanned to have the softness and durability necessary for clothing manufacture.

Glazed Finish A glossy, smooth sheen imparted to leather by polishing with a glass roller.

Glazed Kid Chrome-tanned goat and kidskin leather which has a glazed finish.

Glove Leather Leather from sheep, lamb, deer, pig, goat and mocha skins which are used for dress gloves; horsehides, cattlehide splits, calfskins, sheepskins and pigskins are used for work gloves.

Goatskin Skin or leather of a mature goat.

Grain The hair side of a skin, or the pattern of hair follicles under the epidermis.

Grained Leather Any leather whose natural grain has been highlighted by finishing.

Hair-on Leather Skins or hides tanned without removing the hair.

Harness Leather Curried vegetable-tanned cattlehide which is made quite strong for heavy use.

Hat Leather Sheep or calfskin used in sweatbands.

Head Part of hide cut off at flare into shoulder, sold separately.

Heavy Leather Vegetable-tanned unsplit cattlehide, used for sole, belt and strap leathers.

Hemlock Leather An old-fashioned tanning method which produces a reddish sole leather.

Hide The whole pelt of a large, mature animal (cattlehide, horsehide, etc.).

Horsehide Leather made from horses or colts.

Iron A term used in measuring thickness of leather: one iron = 1/48 inch (one ounce = 1/64 inch).

Kangaroo Leather The strongest known leather weight for weight. It is the chrome-tanned, glazed hide of the Australian kangaroo.

Kid The chrome-tanned skin of a goat or kid.

Kip Skin from an animal of the bovine species between the size of a calf and the mature animal.

Kosher Hide Hide of an animal which has been slaughtered according to Orthodox Hebrew tradition of having the throat cut.

Lace Leather Special rawhide, or alum and oil, chrome or combination-tanned leather, made into long strips, or lacing.

Lambskin Leather Leather made from both lamb and sheepskins.

Larrigan Leather Light, oil-tanned hides, used for moccasins.

Latigo Leather A soft, slightly stretchy, chrome tanned cowhide, 3 to 8-ounce, having a distinct grey stripe in the middle.

Leather The hide or skin of any animal which has been preserved and finished for use.

Levant Goat, sheep or seal skins which are shrunk in tannage to give a grain pattern.

Lining Leather Leather from sheep, kid, goat, cattle, kip or split used to make shoe linings.

Lizard Leather Chrome-tanned lizard skins with fine pattern of scales.

Machine Buff That cut of a hide from which a buffing of 1/64 inch (one ounce) in thickness has been removed from the grain.

Mineral Tan Leather-tanned with chromium salts, alum or other mineral agents, as opposed to vegetable tannages.

Mocha Leather and Suede The former is produced from sheepskin, the grain of which is removed by liming. The fibers below are sueded. The latter is treated the same, but is sueded on the flesh side.

Morocco Leather A distinctive grain of vegetable-tanned goatskin produced by boarding or graining.

Mouton A sheepskin shearling tanned and finished to look like a fur skin.

Nap Finish A process by which a leather's grain layer is removed and the under layer sueded.

Native Hides Bovine hides which are free of brands.

Oak Tan A vegetable tanning process employing oak bark as the agent.

Offal Parts of the hide which are not tanned, or which are made into inferior leather (head, shanks, etc.).

Oil Tan A tanning process which commonly uses fish oils. Strong, light leather is obtained.

Ostrich A leather which is quite thin and fine-grained. It has nodules where the feathers grew.

Ounce In the leather trade, one ounce = 1/64 inch. A measure of thickness, one square foot of 4-ounce leather is supposed to weigh 4 ounces.

Parchment Partially tanned sheepskins.

Patent Leather A leather with a glossy varnish finish.

Peccary A chrome-tanned, washable leather which is very fine and can be split quite thin. It comes from a Mexican wild boar.

Pickling Soaking raw skins in a salt and sulfuric acid solution, which is the initial preservative step in leathermaking.

Pigment Finish An opaque leather finishing material.

Pigskin Leather The vegetable or chrome-tanned skin of pigs, used for dress and work gloves. Hair follicle holes pierce the skin.

Plating The development of a smooth, shiny surface by a plate applied with heat and pressure.

Rawhide Dehaired and limed (partially tanned) cattlehide which is stuffed with oil or grease.

Retanned Leather Leather which is tanned with one agent, then again with another agent to give best qualities of both treatments.

Reversed Calf A heavy, napped, water-resistant calfskin which is stuffed with oils and finished on flesh side.

Saddle Leather Tan-colored vegetable-tanned cowhide used in harness and saddle manufacture.

Shank Part of the hide which was the leg of the animal.

Sharkskin Skin of the shark, vegetable tanned, very rough.

Shearling Sheep or lambskins which were sheared before slaughter. The remaining short hair is left on in tanning.

Shell A kidney-shaped portion from the hindquarters of a horse which yields superior leather.

Shoe Leather Leathers of nearly all weights, from many animals, used in various parts of shoes.

Shoulder Part of hide between neck and main body of hide. Bought separately, it is quite rectangular.

Side Leather One half of a hide, divided along the backbone.

Skin Pelt from a young or small animal (calf, goat, sheep).

Skive To thin down, by paring, a piece of leather. This often aids in joining two pieces.

Skiver The thin, vegetable-tanned grain side split of a sheepskin, used for linings, bookbindings and fancy leathers.

Slunk The skin of an unborn calf.

Snuffed Finish Leather from which the grain has been lightly removed with an emery wheel.

Snuffed Top Grain Upholstery leather of the same type as full top grain, except that the grain has been lightly snuffed.

Sole Ten to twelve-ounce vegetable-tanned cowhide used for outer shoe soles.

Solvent Tannage A tanning system utilizing organic solvents such as acetone in place of aqueous solution to carry the tanning agents.

Split The under portion of a hide or skin which is divided into two or more layers.

Staking The manual or mechanical softening of a leather by working it over a blunt stake.

Steerhide Heavy leather made from the hide of steers.

Stuffed Leather into which wax or grease has been worked.

Suede Finish A finish (*not* a *type* of leather) produced by separating the fibers, giving the leather a nap by abrading with sandpaper or emery wheel.

Syntan Any of several synthetic tanning agents.

Tanning The conversion of a raw animal skin to a stable, workable, long-lasting material.

Tawing An old English term for alum tanning.

Top Grain The grain side of a cattlehide from which splits have been cut.

Traveling Bag Leather A general term for leather used in traveling bags and suitcases.

Unhairing The removal of hair, hair roots and epidermis.

Upholstery Leather A general term used for leather for furniture and upholstery in airplanes, buses and automobiles.

Vegetable Tanning A generic term distinguishing the process of making leather by the use of tannins obtained from bark, wood and other plant and tree parts.

Wallaby Leather Leather from a medium-sized species of kangaroo.

Walrus An extremely thick leather, used most often for buffing wheels.

Washable Leather Leather which may be washed without losing shape, flexibility or color.

Water Repellent Leather Leather which is stuffed with oil, grease or chemical compounds to minimize absorption of H_2O.

Wax Finish Heavy leathers, finished by working wax into flesh side.

Woolskins Sheepskins tanned with the wool on.

List of Suppliers

Listed below are a few of the many suppliers of leathers, tools and materials. You can often find other companies which are closer or more convenient through a local telephone directory, or through the *Thomas Register* at the public library, which lists suppliers by city.

Buy locally when possible, so that you can select the items in person. Hardware stores and supply houses often carry many tools for working with leather and local retail leather goods shops and especially shoe repair shops sometimes sell leather and supplies.

CEMENT
Barge Cement Manufacturing Company, *100 Jacksonville Road, Towaco, New Jersey 07082.*
Borden Chemical Company, *New York, New York.*
R-H Products Company, Inc., *South Acton, Massachusetts.*
Speed-O-Magic, Inc., *1122 Myrtle Avenue, Brooklyn, New York 11206.*

DYE
Fiebing Chemical Company, *Milwaukee, Wisconsin.*
Omega Leathercraft Products Company, Division of Omega Chemical Company, *Fort Worth, Texas.*

FINDINGS AND BUCKLES
Allens Manufacturing Company, Inc., *Providence, Rhode Island.*
American Shoe Specialties Company, Inc., *318 W. 39 Street, New York, New York 10018.*
Basic Bronze & Buckle Bunch, *Box 116, Cerrillos, New Mexico 87010.*
Berman Leather Company, *104 South Street, Boston, Massachusetts 02111.*
The Brass Works, *P.O. Box 66118, Los Angeles, California 90066.*
California Crafts Supply, *1096 North Main, Orange, California.*
Century Leather Company, *Beach Street, Boston, Massachusetts 02111.*
Covert Manufacturing Company, *Troy, New York.*
Drake Leather Company, *3500 West Beverly Boulevard, Montebello, California.*
Flanagan Saddlery Hardware Corporation, *56 Cypress Road, Dumont, New Jersey 07628.*

W. W. Gleckner & Sons Company, *Box 175, Canton, Pennsylvania 17724.*
Handy Ormond Manufacturing Company, Inc., *50-05 47th Avenue, Woodside, New York 11377.*
D. D. Holiday Leather Company, *100 Carver Street, St. Augustine, Florida 32084.*
Indiana Leather & Supply, *R.D. #2, Bloomington, Indiana 47401.*
Just Brass Inc., *1612 Decatur Street, Dept. CH1, Ridgewood, New York 11227.*
North & Judd, *New Britain, Connecticut.*
Russo Leather & Findings, *Los Angeles, California.*
M. Siegel Leather Company, *186 South Street, Boston, Massachusetts 02111.*
Southwestern Leather & Findings, *Phoenix, Arizona.*
Trinity Buckle Company, *P.O. Box 5169, Santa Monica, California 90405.*

LEATHER
August Barth Leather Company, *P.O. Box 88, New Albany, Indiana 47150* (lace leather).
Berman Leather Company, *104 South Street, Boston, Massachusetts 02111* (all supplies).
Caldwell Lace Leather Company, *Auburn, Kentucky.*
California Crafts Supply, *1096 North Main, Orange, California* (all supplies).
Cayadutta Tanning Company, Inc., *Gloversville, New York* (garment leather).
Century Leather Company, *Beach Street, Boston, Massachusetts 02111.*
Cleveland Leather Company, *2824 Lorain Avenue, Cleveland, Ohio 44113.*
Colo-Craft, *Denver, Colorado.*
Colorado Saddlery Company, *Denver, Colorado.*
Creative Leather Workshop, Inc., *12 Bow Street, Harvard Square, Cambridge, Massachusetts 02138.*
Drake Leather Company, *3500 West Beverly Boulevard, Montebello, California* (all supplies).
S. H. Frank Company, *San Francisco, California.*
Hermes Leather Company, *45 W. 34 Street, New York, New York.*
D. D. Holiday Leather Company, *100 Carver Street, St. Augustine, Florida 32084* (leather and tools).
Holser Leather Company, *San Diego, California.*
Indiana Leather & Supply, *R.D. #2, Bloomington, Indiana 47401* (leather, tools, findings).

Jerry's Leather Goods, *Denver, Colorado.*

Lackawanna Leather Company, *7 W. 19 Street, New York, New York.*

MacPherson Leather Company, *200 South Los Angeles Street, Los Angeles, California* (all supplies).

Montana Leather Company, *Butte, Montana.*

New Mexico Leather Company, *1300 2nd N.W., Albuquerque, New Mexico.*

Oregon Leather Company, *Portland, Oregon.*

Pacific Hide & Leather, *Los Angeles, California* (all supplies).

Perkies, Inc., *Kellog Boulevard, St. Paul, Minnesota.*

Potts-Longhorn Company, *Dallas, Texas.*

J. G. Read Company, *Ogden, Utah.*

Russo Leather & Findings, *Los Angeles, California.*

M. Siegel Leather Company, *186 South Street, Boston, Massachusetts 02111.*

Sierra Pine Tanning Company, *3001 Sierra Pine, Vernon, California 90023.*

Skora Supply, *Tucson, Arizona.*

Smith's Leather Shop, *Cedar Avenue, Minneapolis, Minnesota 55404.*

Southwestern Leather & Findings, *Phoenix, Arizona.*

Tucson Leather Company, *Tucson, Arizona.*

MACHINERY

Landis Shoe Machinery Division, Fayscott-Landis Machine Corporation, *5539 Jennings Road, St. Louis, Missouri.*

Sutton Shoe Machinery Company, *P.O. Box 9940, St. Louis, Missouri 63122.*

SOLES AND HEELS

American Biltrite Rubber Company, Inc., *Chelsea, Massachusetts 02150.*

Cat's Paw Rubber Company, Inc., *Baltimore, Maryland 21230.*

O'Sullivan Corporation, *Winchester, Virginia.*

THREAD

American Thread Company, Industrial Division, *High Ridge Park, Stamford, Connecticut 06905.*

Indian Head Yarn & Thread, *Blue Mountain, Alabama 36201.*

Penn Associates, *Philadelphia, Pennsylvania* (waxed linen).

Robinson Thread Company, Inc., *19 McKeon Road, Worcester, Massachusetts 01608.*

TOOLS AND OTHER SUPPLIES (DYE, LACE, ETC.)

Berman Leather Company, *104 South Street, Boston, Massachusetts 02111.*

California Crafts Supply, *1096 North Main, Orange, California.*

Century Leather Company, *Beach Street, Boston, Massachusetts 02111.*

Drake Leather Company, *3500 West Beverly Boulevard, Montebello, California.*

D. D. Holiday Leather Company, *100 Carver Street, St. Augustine, Florida 32084.*

Indiana Leather & Supply, *R.D. #2, Bloomington, Indiana 47401.*

MacPherson Leather Company, *200 South Los Angeles Street, Los Angeles, California.*

C. S. Osborne & Company, *Harrison, New Jersey* (fine tools).

M. Siegel Leather Company, *186 South Street, Boston, Massachusetts 02111.*

Walsall Saddlery Hardware Company, *New York, New York.*

Warren Cutlery, Inc., *P.O. Box 289, Rhinebeck, New York 12572* (knives).

Selling Leather Goods

Every leatherworker I've ever spoken with started out by making something for himself—sandals, a bag, a suitcase, leather pants. Then he began to make gifts for close friends, then Christmas presents for the family. Most stayed with this involvement, making leather goods, sometimes of excellent quality, strictly for pleasure. While their craftsmanship may have been excellent, they had found an involvement with which they were comfortable. The production of beautiful leather goods for yourself and friends can be rewarding indeed. Some went further, however, and began selling their goods. You may wish to do the same.

Selling is an art in itself. Basically, there are three types of selling: consignment (consigned risk), wholesale and retail; each having different advantages and disadvantages and each requiring a different approach.

When you *consign* goods, it means you give them to a retailer to sell for you. He places them among his wares, where they rest until they are sold. *You* take the risk, not the retailer. *Your* money and material are tied up on the shelf until the right buyer comes along. Who's to guarantee the goods won't get stained or faded and who will reimburse you if they get lost or stolen? No one; it's your loss! Not only that, but you must keep track of the goods and call or run over to check them from time to time. However, a redeeming factor is that consignment selling provides you with an outlet which you wouldn't have otherwise. Also, you get a higher percentage—about 70 percent—of the selling price than with any other arrangement. (Remember, though, that the retailer would rather sell an item from which he gets 50 percent than one he gets only 30 percent.)

Wholesaling goods means that you sell goods directly to the retailer, or commercial outlet. You are his supplier. In this type of selling, you get approximately 50 percent of the retail price, since the retailer takes all the risks. With this arrangement, if an item is lost, stolen or sat on, it is his loss. While you're making 20 percent less, the advantage is that the goods are sold, not waiting to be sold; the money is in your pocket and you're out the door. Maybe a local gift shop would be interested in your handbags or a small men's shop may want wallets and belts. Prepare a sample case and talk to the manager. If you wholesale on a large enough scale, you eventually may hire a salesman. His salary cuts your profit, but increases your sales and your time to work. A buyer may want an exclusive on your work. That means he doesn't want you to sell to anyone else in town. Respect this request. One good buyer is better than two poor ones.

Your wholesaling will probably go one of two ways. It will be either a one-shot deal where the retailer misjudged the demand and later puts your work on sale, or your work may go over very well. This second situation should not be taken lightly, nor should wholesaling in general. The retailer's business is to sell and if your goods go well, he'll want or even demand more of the same. You are bound to keep him supplied, more often by unwritten code than by contract. Be ready to produce.

Retailing means setting up shop and selling goods yourself and is an extremely tricky, sometimes lucrative, business. When you retail goods, you receive 100 percent of the selling price. Fine. But then out of this 100 percent comes X percent for lights, heat, salaries, raw materials, rent and other overhead charges. By carefully balancing money coming in and money going out, you determine your profit margin. Out of that 100 percent, your profit may be 20 percent. And this may well get plowed back into the store, leaving you only enough to eat with. Retailing on a professional level is much too complex to go into here. I refer you to a pamphlet, "The Handcraft Business," Small Business Reporter, Bank of America, Dept. 3102, P.O. Box 37000, San Francisco, California 94137 ($1). Another publication, "Encouraging American Craftsmen," is an excellent informational resource for all types of production and marketing of crafts. Write Superintendent of Documents, U.S. Government Printing Office, Washington, D.C. 20402 (45¢).

Retailing can also be done on a semi-professional level, with much less trouble and investment, but also less return or profit. You can retail your goods at craft fairs, bazaars and shows. These fairs are held in most parts of the country all summer long and are getting more popular and better attended every year. A list of fairs in your area can probably be obtained from your local or county chamber of commerce. While you're retailing your own goods at these fairs, you may also sell some friends' things on consignment. Remember—it's their risk—and varied displays attract more customers.

At least two craftsmen I know make their livings by producing work all winter and selling it and taking orders all summer at craft fairs. Participating in fairs is a very enjoyable way to sell, learn and meet other craftsmen. Exchanging views on your craft keeps you well-rounded, as does examining other people's work. Craftsmen are generally willing to swap goods—a batik for a belt, a wallhanging for a white handbag. This is fun and a fine way to do business.

Whatever system you use to sell your goods, you will need to price them. Handmade things are hard to price. Their value depends on the cost of the original material and the skill of the artisan. There are several pricing formulas for various types of crafts. The one which I've found best suited to leatherwork is this:

Cost of materials + your hourly wage (which increases with your skill) + 20 percent for waste.

A good-sized purse using about 4 to 5-square feet of leather can take 4 to 5 hours to make, especially if it is an original design. If the leather costs you $1.50 per foot (including shipping), you've put in about $6 to $8 in leather alone. Add findings—about $1 to $1.50. With a starting salary of $1.50 to $2.00 per hour, you allow yourself about $8 in wages. Add 20 percent waste and you have a bag which you can't afford to wholesale at under $16 to $18. This purse will retail at $35. At this price, unless it is very good it may not sell. (Note that a poorly made purse uses the same amount of material as a well-made one.) You can reduce your costs to the consumer by reducing your own costs: buy good leather at the lowest price (don't stoop to lessening the quality of your material), use your leather *and scrap* efficiently and utilize your time to the best advantage.

Besides this complex formula, there is another, easier, pricing system: comparison pricing. You can assume that a bag will sell at $12 to $25, depending on size and quality. A $40 bag is either selling in a major city or is a masterpiece. A belt sells for $5 to $8. Again, a $14 belt has got to be pretty special. Compare your prices with those in a good, professional leather shop. Your prices should run accordingly, but preferably on the low side. You don't have the overhead they do and they have the skills and artistry which you may one day develop. Be aware that underpricing is not going to make you overwhelmingly popular in that shop.

140

Bibliography

Adams, Jeanette T. and Emanuele Stieri: *The Complete Woodworking Handbook*, Arco Publishing Company, Inc., New York, 1960.

Ashbrook, Frank G.: *Furs, Glamorous and Practical—Fur Buying Mystery Removed*, Van Nostrand Company, Inc., New York, 1954.

Ashley, Clifford W.: *The Ashley Book of Knots*, Doubleday, Doran & Company, Inc., Garden City, New York, 1945.

Cherry, Raymond: *General Leathercraft*, McKnight and McKnight, Bloomington, Illinois, 1949.

Close, Eunice: *How to Make Gloves*, Charles T. Branford Company, Boston, 1950.

Dean, John W.: *Leathercraft Techniques and Designs*, McKnight and McKnight, Bloomington, Illinois, 1950.

Encyclopedia Americana: "Tannic Acid," International Edition, Vol. 26, Americana Corp., New York, 1971.

Farnham, A. B.: *Home Tanning and Leather Making Guide*, A. R. Harding Publishing Company, Columbus, Ohio, 1950.

Grant, Bruce: *How to Make Cowboy Horse Gear*, Cornell Maritime Press, Inc., Cambridge, Maryland, 1956.

———: *Leather Braiding*, Cornell Maritime Press, Inc., Cambridge, Maryland, 1961.

Home Manufacture of Furs and Skins, available through Fur, Fish, Game, 2878 E. Main Street, Columbus, Ohio.

Karg, Henry: *Shoe Repairing*, Bruce Publishing Company, Milwaukee, Wisconsin, 1965.

Klingsmith, Willey P.: *Leatherwork Procedure and Design*, Bruce Publishing Company, Milwaukee, Wisconsin, 1958.

Lobel, The Brothers: *Meat*, Hawthorne Books, Inc., New York, 1971.

Peterson, Grete: *Creative Leathercraft*, Sterling Publishing Company, New York, 1960.

Thorstensen, Thomas C.: *Practical Leather Technology*, Van Nostrand Reinhold Company, New York, 1969.

University of the State of New York, The: *Studio in Art*, Albany, New York, 1966.

Waring, Ralph G.: *Modern Wood Finishing*, Bruce Publishing Company, Milwaukee, Wisconsin, 1963.

Waterer, John W.: *A Guide to the Conservation and Restoration of Objects Made Wholly or in Part of Leather*, Drake Publishers, Inc., New York, 1972.

———: *Leather Craftsmanship*, Fredric A. Praeger Publishing Company, New York, 1968.

Willcox, Donald: *Modern Leather Design*, Watson-Guptill Publications, New York, 1969.

Index

150

Steven Edwards

I was born and raised in Rochester, N. Y. I majored in art in high school. Upon graduation from high school, I enrolled in Tyler School of Art of Temple University, Philadelphia, Pennsylvania. I majored in sculpture and ceramics and graduated with a B.F.A. I spent my third year in Rome, Italy, in Temple Abroad, Tyler's Rome branch.

Also while in college, I worked at a leather shop in Philadelphia, making sandals. In my senior year, I did custom-made handbags independently and sold to various shops in Philadelphia and Rochester.

After graduation from Tyler, I came to Clayton, New York, a village directly on the St. Lawrence River, where my wife Nancy, a weaver, our son and I now reside. I have taught ceramics and leather at the Thousand Islands Museum Craft School here in Clayton. I also taught for a year as a program specialist in leather for Community Action Planning Council, a social agency. In this position, I designed, developed, taught and administrated leather workshops. I am presently employed as a junior high school art teacher and an independent craftsman.